MW00607974

OLD TIME HAWKEY'S
RECIPES FROM THE CEDAR SWAMP

OLD TIME HAWKEY'S
RECIPES FROM THE CEDAR SWAMP

Publisher Mike Sanders
Art & Design Director William Thomas
Editorial Director Ann Barton
Senior Editor Olivia Peluso
Designer Lindsay Dobbs
Photographer Kelley Jordan Schuyler
Illustrator Logan Schmitt
Food Stylist Lovoni Walker
Recipe Tester Ashley Brooks
Proofreaders Christina Guthrie & Lisa Himes
Indexer Louisa Emmons

First American Edition, 2024
Published in the United States by DK Publishing
1745 Broadway, 20th Floor, New York, NY 10019

The authorized representative in the EEA is Dorling
Kindersley Verlag GmbH. Arnulfstr. 124, 80636 Munich,
Germany

Copyright © 2024 by Old Time Hawkey
DK, a Division of Penguin Random House LLC
23 24 25 26 27 10 9 8 7 6 5 4 3 2 1
001–339649–May/2024

All rights reserved.
Without limiting the rights under the copyright reserved
above, no part of this publication may be reproduced, stored
in or introduced into a retrieval system, or transmitted, in any
form, or by any means (electronic, mechanical, photocopying,
recording, or otherwise), without the prior written
permission of the copyright owner.

A catalog record for this book
is available from the Library of Congress.
ISBN 978-0-7440-9390-2

DK books are available at special discounts when purchased
in bulk for sales promotions, premiums, fund-raising, or
educational use. For details, contact SpecialSales@dk.com

Printed and bound in China
www.dk.com

MIX
Paper | Supporting
responsible forestry
FSC™ C018179

This book was made with Forest
Stewardship Council™ certified
paper – one small step in DK's
commitment to a sustainable future.
Learn more at
www.dk.com/uk/information/sustainability

DEDICATED
TO YOU, BUDDY.

CONTENTS

Dutch Oven

Pudgy Pies

Foil Packs

COMPANIONS

Appetizers

Desserts

Drinks

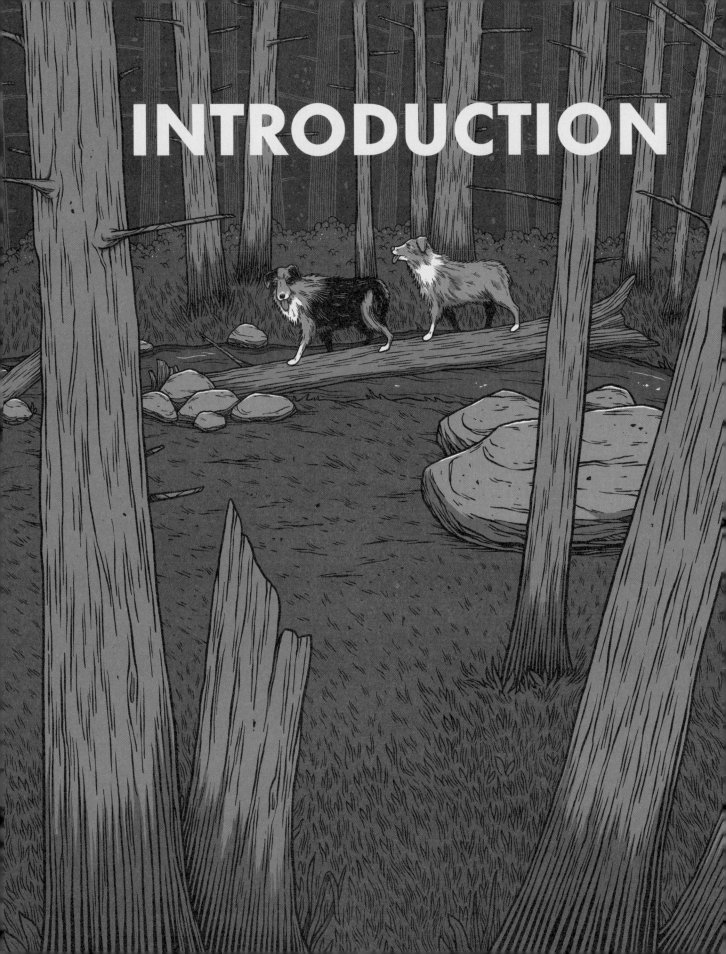

INTRODUCTION

THE CEDAR SWAMP

"Come here, boys!" I yell into the dense cedar swamp. The only response is the mating call of a black-capped chickadee, which, if you listen closely, sounds a lot like "hey sweetie." I yell again, "Come here, boys!" and clap my hands three times.

Between two birch trees, softened by the rain and bent by the wind, emerges my eleven-year-old blue merle Australian Shepherd, Donnybrook. He's named after the hockey term for a brawl or multiple fights during a game. His fur is four colors—grey, white, brown, and black—and all the colors are fighting each other. His younger brother, somewhere nearby, is a two-year-old red merle Australian Shepherd named Kris Draper, after one of my favorite Detroit Red Wings players, who also has red hair and piercing blue eyes. Together, we are known to millions as Old Time Hawkey. But here among the pine martens, the white-tailed deer, and even the blue-spotted salamanders, we're just a couple of travelers on our own journey. A journey that began over thirty years ago in this very cedar swamp, when I was a young child running alongside the creek banks, trying to lure clearwater crayfish into a pan with a stick.

Growing up here, I learned to be patient from the slow-growing oaks. I learned how to adapt from the creek's steady current, which forged its way through the ground, around logs and rocks, through steep valleys, bridges, and dams. Everything else I learned from my grandfather, who bought this land in the 1950s.

In the late fall of 1994, on our way to inspect whitetail scrapes near his hunting spot, he taught me how to cook the perfect pudgy pie over an open fire, with the sun barely peeking over the pines. He opened his weathered knapsack and pulled out his old cast pie iron, a couple worn mason jars, and a folded hand towel containing homemade brioche bread. Using the ridge of his compass, which I still keep with me today, he pressed a hole in the center of one of the bread slices and cracked an egg inside it. After a healthy palm of pepper and salt, and a slice of American cheese, he closed the clamp of the pie iron, smiled at me, and placed it over the white coals. As the fire went to work, my grandfather and I did the exact opposite: We just sat there and took it all in.

Today, almost thirty years later, three river rocks mark this exact spot. I find myself here often in the fall, thinking about that cheesy Egg in a Hole Pudgy Pie, surrounded by saplings I've never met, yet our grandfathers knew each other well.

Everyone has a "cedar swamp." However, not everyone's cedar swamp is a wooded marshland. It could be a childhood home, an old journal, or something as simple as a scent or an old song. A place where the past meets the present. A place that is untouched by time. Revisiting these places, both physically and mentally, reminds us that amidst the chaos and change, a part of us will always remain the same. This is mine—simple recipes inspired by three generations of campfires, deer camps, and family gatherings spent here in Northern Michigan.

HOW TO USE THIS BOOK

I've divided this book into three sections: Indoor, Campfire, and Companions. Each section offers a unique adventure and features recipes that can be made in the comfort of your own home, over an open flame, or as a delightful addition to any main course.

INDOOR

The indoor section includes plenty of hearty soups and stews, classic comfort foods, innovative casseroles, and a variety of pancakes and toasts. Cooking these recipes will require basic kitchen equipment like pots and pans, cutting boards, knives, spatulas, and wooden spoons. You'll also need a slow cooker for the recipes in the slow cooker chapter (starting on page 85).

A well-stocked pantry is a cook's best friend. Keeping a variety of spices, oils, and baking essentials like flour, sugar, baking powder, and brown sugar on hand ensures that you're always prepared to whip up a delicious meal.

When cooking indoors, try to elevate the vibe by playing your favorite movie, music, or even an old classic video game. Consider using lanterns to create a sense of comfort, and try using vintage cookware that not only holds sentimental value but is also no stranger to a delicious, hot-cooked meal. Efficiency is important: Having your ingredients premeasured can save time and stress. Imagine small wooden bowls filled with these prepared ingredients, and spice jars clearly labeled, all organized and ready for use. The French refer to this as mise en place, which means "everything in its place." This is a fundamental practice in professional kitchens and is extremely helpful for cooking at home as well. It's not only visually appealing but it also streamlines the cooking process and minimizes mistakes.

The combination of a pleasant atmosphere, thoughtful preparation, and a well-stocked pantry can turn cooking indoors into a wonderful experience, filled with warm memories and plenty of delicious meals.

CAMPFIRE

Cooking over a campfire is a great way to cook and enjoy a meal, but it does require some more preparation and the right equipment. Cast-iron skillets, a Dutch oven, and grill grates are solid investments that can withstand high heat and distribute it evenly. Long-handled utensils like skewers are ideal for grilling meats or roasting marshmallows, while keeping your hands safe and away from the heat. And please don't forget—to handle cookware safely, an old leather hockey glove works great as a mitt, but you can also use some heat resistant gloves or utensils. Safety is paramount, so always have water or a fire extinguisher nearby, and never leave your campfire unattended.

The key to a delicious campfire meal is creating the perfect fire. Choose a flat, open spot away from trees, bushes, and flammable materials. Make a ring with large rocks to contain the fire. Start with a large pile of dry sticks, twigs, and larger pieces for the fire and to use later for fuel. Begin your fire with dry wood and allow it to burn down to hot coals for even, consistent heat. Flames look pretty cool but are less predictable and can burn your food. Use different zones of the fire for cooking: hotter coals for searing and cooler spots for slow cooking. Remember to rotate your food or stir it occasionally for even cooking.

When cooking on a campfire, or in general, remember our French buddies and their philosophy of mise en place, where "everything is in its place." Keep your cooking area clean and well organized, with separate areas for food prep and cooking.

COMPANIONS

The Companions section features appetizers, desserts, and drinks that can be enjoyed by themselves or as "companions" to a larger meal. These recipes are perfect for sharing with loved ones or for savoring alone, paired with a good book, video game, or movie. To prepare them, you will need a variety of kitchen equipment: a slow cooker, blender, pots and pans, baking sheets, a whisk, spoons and ladles, and a couple of reliable vessels for serving both hot and cold drinks.

These recipes may not be the main course, but that doesn't make them any less significant. Pairing the right dessert to follow supper can tie the bow on a very special night. A hot drink can contrast the coldest of temperatures. And there's no better way to break the ice and get into a few heart-to-hearts over delicious appetizers with a couple of cold pops.

Companion dishes can also be prepared for special events, like potlucks, theme parties, sporting events, or large gatherings where dishes are passed. In these cases, you may need to consider how to keep your dishes hot or cold. A well-insulated cooler, thermos, or ice-bottomed dish can keep cold dishes fresh or drinks cold. A slow cooker, insulated carafe, portable stove, or hot plate can keep hot dishes warm and steamy.

Have fun pairing your companion dishes with events by using the theme, holiday, or occasion as inspiration. For example, serve my Taco Dip recipe (on page 199) on "Taco Tuesday" along with local artisan tortilla chips. Or bring a slow cooker filled with Hug in a Mug (on page 236) to the company holiday party, complete with marshmallows, peppermint sticks, and vintage mugs for enjoyment!

INDOOR

INDOOR

"Does everyone have what they need?" my mother would always ask, standing close to the dinner table where she was ready to serve. She would make sure everyone had a cold (or hot)drink, while gazing around at our plates to ensure we had proper portions—all habits that were passed down from my grandmother. They both believed that serving a meal with a warm smile and heartfelt hospitality was as crucial to the meal as the food itself.

When I was growing up, my mother worked as a waitress at a local restaurant in town. It was a place where everyone gathered to smoke cigarettes, drink coffee, and enjoy a good meal. The front counter stools were consistently packed with "regulars" from all walks of life. As a child, I was impressed by the symphony behind the scenes, where the kitchen (known as the back of the house), and the dining area (where waiters like my mother worked), collaborated to provide a quality dining experience for the customers. Just like at our dinner table at home, the hospitality my mother displayed was as essential to the process as seasoning or cooking the food.

These indoor recipes take me back to quiet weeknights filled with the gentle sounds of my mother in the kitchen: pans scraping, the radio playing, and the faucet running. The sweet smells of supper engulfing our small home, signaling that it was almost time to sit down at the dinner table and eat. For us, the dinner table was where life's biggest and simplest moments came together. It was where we started each day quietly over breakfast, and where we finished each day eating supper and talking about our days. And the story of each meal's creation was always part of the conversation. Whether it was a family recipe passed down through generations, a new dish born from an experiment, or a simple comfort food, each meal had its own narrative. Just as my mother's cooking brought our family together, I hope these recipes bring you the same comfort and warmth that good company provides, whether you're with others or alone, and no matter where your dinner table might be.

For some, a dinner table might be a well-crafted piece of wood, large enough to accommodate extended family. For others, maybe it's a small, intimate table for two, nestled in a cozy kitchen, perfect for a quiet meal. In the busy city, it could be a small foldable table, easy to set up and put away, or even a countertop that doubles as a dining area. For students, the dinner table might be a temporary setup on a coffee table or a desk, where textbooks and laptops vie for space with old pizza boxes, plates, and cups. But whatever your dinner table is, I hope these recipes remind you of the importance of taking a moment to appreciate the simple joys in life—like the taste of a well-cooked meal, the comfort of good company, or the peace and quiet of a delicious meal alone. The most meaningful connections are made when we simply sit down and eat a good meal.

Cheers, buddy.

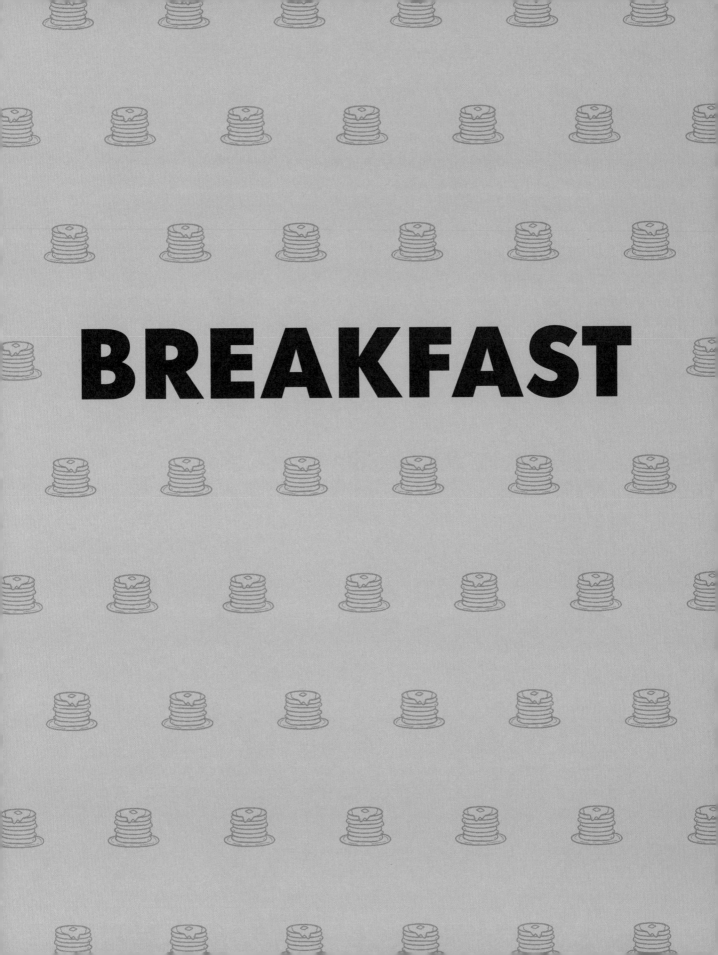

BREAKFAST

PUMPKIN PANCAKES

Throw on your best flannel and take your taste buds on a ride through a pumpkin patch with this year-round recipe. These pancakes are perfect for breakfast, brunch, or a sweet supper. Complement the natural sweetness of the pumpkin with a drizzle of all-natural grade A tree juice.

SERVES 2 TO 3

1¼ cups cake flour
2 tablespoons light brown sugar
2 teaspoons baking powder
1 teaspoon ground cinnamon
¼ teaspoon kosher salt
¼ teaspoon ground nutmeg
¼ teaspoon ground ginger
⅛ teaspoon allspice
1 cup buttermilk
½ cup canned pumpkin
1 large egg
2 tablespoons melted butter
1 teaspoon vanilla extract
Nonstick cooking spray

Serving Suggestions

Butter and grade A tree juice
   (maple syrup)
Whipped cream and pecans
Greek yogurt, granola, and fresh fruit

1 In a medium bowl, whisk the cake flour, brown sugar, baking powder, cinnamon, salt, nutmeg, ginger, and allspice. Then, set aside.

2 In a large bowl, whisk your buttermilk, pumpkin, egg, butter, and vanilla.

3 Add the dry ingredients to the wet ingredients and stir without overmixing the batter. Lumps are fine.

4 Heat a 10-inch skillet over medium heat or an electric griddle to 350°F.

5 Coat your skillet or griddle with cooking spray. Pour about ⅓ cup of batter into the pan. Wait until the edges of the pancakes look dry and bubbles start to appear and then burst, 2 to 3 minutes. Use a thin spatula to flip, then cook until golden brown, another 2 to 3 minutes.

6 Serve the pancakes with butter and plenty of grade A tree juice, a dollop of whipped cream and pecans, or a spoon of Greek yogurt, granola, and some fresh fruit for a healthier twist. Enjoy!

THE ULTIMATE BREAKFAST SANDWICH

The ultimate hearty breakfast in between two slices of an everything bagel. When made right, this versatile sandwich is as complex and dense as a healthy house cat.

SERVES 1

3 strips applewood smoked bacon
1 everything bagel
2 tablespoons mayonnaise
1 slice black forest ham
2 large eggs
Handful of fresh baby spinach
1 slice cheddar
1 slice pepper jack
Kosher salt
Black pepper

1 Heat a large skillet over medium heat. Add the bacon and cook until golden brown and crispy, about 8 minutes. Transfer to paper towels to drain. Drain most of the grease from the skillet but leave it coated.

2 Cut the bagel in half and spread mayonnaise on the inside of each half. Add the bagel halves to the skillet, cut side down. Toast over medium heat until golden brown, 3 minutes. Remove and set aside.

3 In the same large skillet, fry the ham on both sides until it's thoroughly heated, about 2 minutes, then set aside.

4 Fry the eggs over medium heat to your desired doneness, 4 to 5 minutes. Add salt and pepper to taste.

5 Now, it's time to put on our hard hats and build. Place the bottom half of the bagel on a plate. Then, top it with the spinach, ham, bacon, pepper jack, cheddar, and fried eggs. Place the other bagel half on top and enjoy!

COWPOKE OMELET

This rugged and simple omelet is best enjoyed on a sturdy tin plate or a chunk of wood. Whether made over a crackling fire or cooked on your stovetop at the homestead, this recipe will make you think you're living on the frontier. Provides a full day's worth of energy for hittin' the old dusty trail.

SERVES 1

3 large eggs
2 tablespoons butter, divided
½ cup finely diced onion
¼ cup finely diced green and red bell peppers
¼ cup cubed cooked ham
¼ cup shredded pepper jack
Pinch of kosher salt
Pinch of black pepper

1   In a medium bowl, beat the eggs with a fork, until no blobs or bubbles are present. Add a pinch of salt and black pepper.

2   Heat a 10-inch skillet over medium-low heat, then add 1 tablespoon of butter and melt, about 1 minute. Add the onion, bell peppers, and ham and cook until the onion and peppers start to soften, 3 to 5 minutes. Remove from the pan and set aside.

3   Melt the other tablespoon of butter in the pan. Pour the eggs into the center of the skillet and use a silicone spatula to stir in a circular motion until the eggs begin to set, 5 to 10 seconds.

4   Move the spatula around the edge to round out the omelet and lift up carefully to loosen the edges and make sure it isn't sticking to the pan.

5   Let the omelet develop an outer crust by cooking it for 10 seconds without touching. Then, add in your onions, bell peppers, and ham.

6   Reduce the heat to low and cover with a lid (see Tip) for 4 to 5 minutes, until the eggs are cooked almost all the way through.

7   Flip the entire omelet and cook until the eggs are cooked through, 1 more minute.

8   Sprinkle the pepper jack on top. Then, fold the omelet into a semicircle and cover again to let the cheese melt inside. Enjoy!

Tip: Use a tempered glass lid if you have one. That way, you can keep an eye on it while it cooks.

SAUSAGE GRAVY & BISCUITS

A staple of my family gatherings, lovingly handed down by my stepfather Mike. This recipe is a great way to slow down the pace of a busy morning. It might not be fancy, but it's a hearty breakfast that I hope reminds you of your favorite local diner. Think mop and a bucket, eh?

SERVES 4 TO 6

Biscuits
2 cups all-purpose flour, plus more for dusting

1 tablespoon baking powder

1 tablespoon light brown sugar

1 teaspoon kosher salt

6 tablespoons (¾ stick) cold unsalted butter, cubed

¾ cup buttermilk

2 tablespoons melted unsalted butter

Gravy
16 ounces ground pork breakfast sausage

⅓ cup all-purpose flour

½ teaspoon kosher salt

1 teaspoon black pepper

¼ teaspoon white pepper

¼ teaspoon cayenne (optional)

3 cups milk

1   Preheat the oven to 425°F. Line a baking sheet with parchment paper.

2   **Make the biscuits:** In a large bowl, whisk the flour, baking powder, brown sugar, and salt. Add the butter. Using a pastry blender, cut the butter into the flour until the mixture resembles coarse crumbs. Then add the buttermilk and stir slowly to form a dough. Be careful not to overmix.

3   Dust a work surface with flour, then turn out the dough. Use your hands to bring the dough together and gently fold it over itself a few times, to form a craggy dough, 2 to 3 minutes. If the dough is too sticky, dust with a little more flour. Flatten the dough to about 1-inch thick.

4   Take a biscuit cutter, cookie cutter, or tin can and press firmly into the dough. Place the cut-out biscuit onto your baking sheet. Repeat until you've fit as many biscuits as possible into a safe neighborhood, about ½ inch apart.

5   Bake for 12 minutes or until the biscuits are golden brown. Remove from the oven, then brush gently with melted butter.

6   **Meanwhile, make the gravy:** Heat a large skillet over medium heat. Add the sausage and cook until browned, 5 to 6 minutes.

7   Add the flour and stir until all the grease from the sausage is absorbed. Then, turn the heat down to low but continue to brown the flour and meat, 2 to 3 more minutes. Add the salt, black pepper, white pepper, and cayenne for an extra kick.

8   Add the milk slowly, about ½ cup at a time, whisking to prevent lumps. Bring the gravy to a simmer, stirring occasionally until it thickens, about 10 minutes. Add more salt and pepper to taste.

9   Split the biscuits in half and top with gravy. Sprinkle with more pepper to taste.

CINNAMON ROLL PANCAKES

These pancakes will transport you back to simpler days. For me, it's back to Boy Scouts and a crisp morning spent camping, or the peace and quiet of a holiday morning. The sound of batter hitting the hot griddle will nudge even the deepest sleeper awake and into the kitchen—even old Uncle Butch.

SERVES 2 TO 4

Cinnamon Filling
¾ cup brown sugar
⅓ cup melted butter
1 tablespoon ground cinnamon

Pancake Batter
1¼ cups cake flour
2 teaspoons baking powder
½ teaspoon kosher salt
1 cup milk
1 tablespoon vegetable oil
1 large egg
Nonstick cooking spray

Cream Cheese Glaze
4 tablespoons (½ stick) butter
2 ounces cream cheese, softened
1¼ cups powdered sugar
1 teaspoon vanilla extract

1 **Make the cinnamon filling:** In a medium bowl, mix the brown sugar, butter, and cinnamon. Scoop the filling into a zipper bag and set aside. Let rest for 15 minutes or until thick.

2 **Make your pancake batter:** In a medium bowl, whisk the cake flour, baking powder, and salt. Whisk in the milk, oil, and egg until the batter is moist and there are no lumps.

3 **Make your cream cheese glaze:** In a medium microwave-safe bowl, microwave the butter and cream cheese until melted, about 30 seconds. Whisk together until smooth, then whisk in the powdered sugar and vanilla. Set aside.

4 Heat a large skillet over low heat or an electric griddle to 250°F. Coat with cooking spray.

5 Pour in about ½ cup of batter. Wait until the edges of the pancakes look dry and bubbles start to appear and then burst, 1 to 2 minutes. Use a thin spatula to flip and cook until golden brown, another 1 to 2 minutes.

6 Snip a corner off your zipper bag with the cinnamon filling. Squeeze a spiral of the filling onto the top of the pancake.

7 Serve each pancake topped with warmed cream cheese glaze and enjoy!

CARAMELIZED BANANA TOAST

Here's an easy recipe to elevate your morning toast. Caramelized bananas atop a peanut butter spread, drizzled with tree juice, and sprinkled with coconut—holy wah! Why are you still reading this, buddy? Go get to work.

SERVES 2

1 banana
2 tablespoons butter
2 slices bread (I prefer whole wheat)
1 tablespoon coconut oil
1 tablespoon grade A tree juice
   (maple syrup)
¼ teaspoon ground cinnamon
¼ teaspoon vanilla extract
¼ cup peanut butter
¼ cup shredded coconut

1   Slice your banana into ¼-inch pieces.

2   Melt the butter in a large pan over medium-high heat. Add the bread and toast for 2 to 3 minutes per side. Remove from the pan.

3   Add your coconut oil, tree juice, cinnamon, and vanilla, then mix well.

4   Add the banana slices to the pan. Create the perfect neighborhood by leaving enough space in between the bananas, so they don't stick to each other.

5   Cook the bananas until they're caramelized to your liking, 3 to 5 minutes on each side. You can check them by using a fork and gently lifting them.

6   Spread half of the peanut butter on one slice of bread. Repeat with the other slice.

7   Add your caramelized banana slices on top and cover with some coconut shreds. Enjoy!

TATER TOT BREAKFAST CASSEROLE

A quick dish that everyone's cool with. A bite of this casserole takes me back to my school days, when tater tots for breakfast fed the entire family. A couple slices of this casserole paired with a giant glass of orange juice—that's everything you need to start the day off right.

SERVES 6 TO 8

Nonstick cooking spray
1 pound ground pork breakfast
  sausage
1 red bell pepper, chopped
1 green bell pepper, chopped
1 medium yellow onion, diced
3 garlic cloves, minced
8 large eggs
2 cups half and half
One 4-ounce can diced green chiles
1 teaspoon dried parsley
½ teaspoon yellow mustard
½ teaspoon chili powder
½ teaspoon dried oregano
½ teaspoon kosher salt
½ teaspoon black pepper
One 32-ounce bag frozen tater tots,
  divided
1½ cups shredded sharp cheddar,
  divided
1½ cups shredded pepper jack,
  divided

For Serving (optional)
Chopped chives
Chopped green onions
Chopped shallots

1 Preheat the oven to 350°F. Coat a 9 x 13-inch casserole dish with cooking spray.

2 Heat a large skillet over medium-high heat and add in your sausage, bell peppers, and onion. Cook until the sausage is browned and the onions are softened, 5 to 7 minutes. Add in the garlic and sauté until fragrant, 30 seconds. Drain the grease and add the mixture to your casserole dish. Then, set aside to cool.

3 In a large bowl, whisk your eggs, half and half, chiles, parsley, mustard, chili powder, dried oregano, salt, and black pepper. Set aside.

4 Add half of the tater tots to your casserole dish and then add ¾ cup each of cheddar and pepper jack. Stir and spread into an even layer.

5 Pour the egg mixture over the tater tots, sausage, and cheese. Then spread the remaining tater tots on top.

6 Bake for 45 to 55 minutes or until the casserole reaches an internal temperature of 160°F.

7 Safely remove the dish from the oven and cover with the remaining ¾ cup each of cheddar and pepper jack. Return to the oven and bake for 5 to 10 minutes, until the cheese is melted.

8 Remove from the oven, serve with chives, green onions, or shallots, and enjoy!

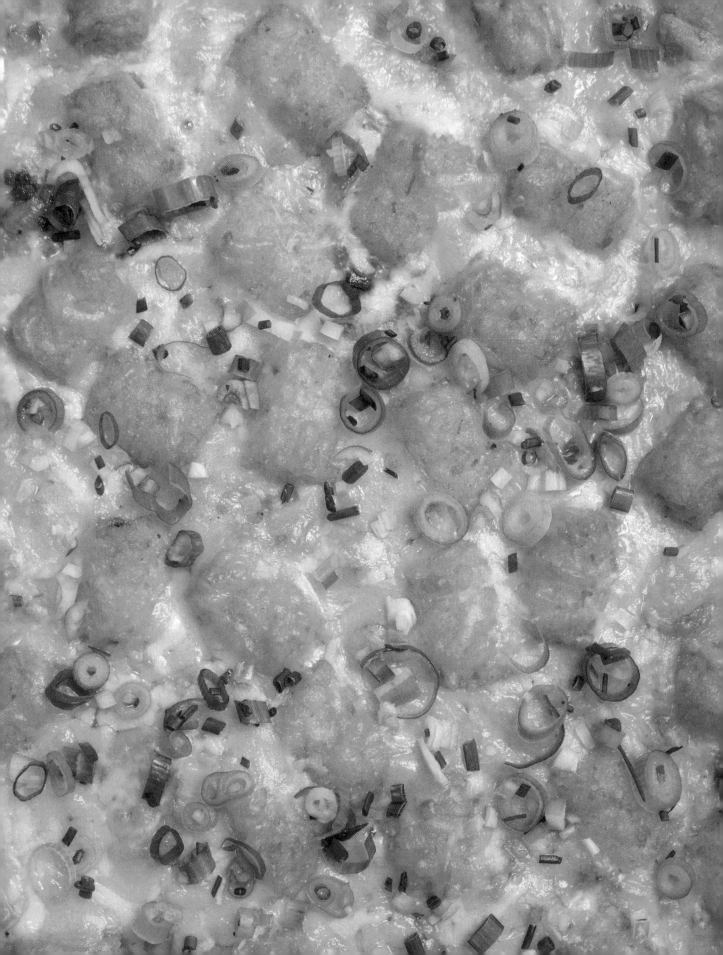

EVERYTHING BAGEL BREAKFAST SLIDERS

Make sure to keep one hand open for handshakes, because you will be the talk of every potluck with these bite-size breakfast sliders. They provide everything you need to fuel your day.

MAKES 10 SLIDERS

Nonstick cooking spray
8 eggs
¼ cup milk
8 slices bacon
Pinch of kosher salt
Pinch of black pepper
10 mini bagels
¼ cup cream cheese
1½ cups shredded cheddar
3 tablespoons melted butter
2 teaspoons granulated garlic
2 teaspoons dried onion
2 teaspoons poppy seeds
2 teaspoons sesame seeds

1 Preheat the oven to 350°F and coat a 9 x 13-inch casserole dish with cooking spray.

2 In a large bowl, beat your eggs and whisk in the milk until the mixture is light and frothy.

3 Heat a 10-inch skillet over medium heat, and cook your bacon until golden brown and crispy, 8 minutes. Transfer the bacon to paper towels to drain. Pour out almost all of the bacon fat, but leave the pan coated.

4 Pour your egg mixture into the skillet and turn down the heat to medium-low. Cook, stirring occasionally, until the eggs are cooked and no longer runny, about 7 minutes. Season with salt and pepper. Remove from the heat.

5 Cut your mini bagels in half and spread cream cheese onto the bottom halves. Place the bagels into the casserole dish and create a safe neighborhood, placing the bagels side by side, with a little room in between them.

6 Evenly distribute your cooked egg, bacon, and cheddar on the bottom half of each bagel. Then add the bagel tops. Brush the bagel tops with melted butter and sprinkle granulated garlic, dried onion, poppy seeds, and sesame seeds on top to make mini everything bagels.

7 Bake for about 10 minutes, until the bagels are toasty and the cheese has melted. Enjoy!

SKILLET FRENCH TOAST & PEACH PRESERVES CASSEROLE

This casserole, topped with pecans and fresh berries, delivers a rich and fruity flavor. It's perfect for a holiday brunch, festive occasion, or simple breakfast treat. It's also an ideal choice for gaining public recognition on various social media platforms.

SERVES 8

3 cups plain yogurt
8 large egg yolks
¼ cup grade A tree juice (maple syrup)
1 tablespoon vanilla extract
¼ teaspoon kosher salt
1 cup peach preserves
8 croissants, torn into large chunks
½ cup chopped pecans
½ cup fresh raspberries
½ cup fresh blackberries

1   Preheat the oven to 350°F.

2   In a large bowl, whisk the yogurt, egg yolks, tree juice, vanilla extract, and salt. Whisk until frothy.

3   Heat the peach preserves in a small saucepan over medium heat until liquidy, 1 to 2 minutes.

4   Arrange half of the croissant pieces on the bottom of a large cast-iron skillet. Drizzle with half of the warmed peach preserves. Pour half of the egg mixture over the croissants.

5   Repeat the process with the remaining croissant pieces, peach preserves, and egg. Lightly press the croissants down to saturate them partially with liquid, but do not submerge them completely. Set aside for 20 to 30 minutes to let them soak before baking.

6   Sprinkle with pecans, raspberries, and blackberries.

7   Cover the skillet with a lid or aluminum foil and bake for 30 minutes. Then, remove the cover and continue cooking for 15 to 20 minutes, until the croissants are golden brown.

8   Let cool for 10 to 15 minutes before serving and enjoy!

CHEESY BREAKFAST QUESADILLA

An early morning calls for a quick and easy breakfast sandwich between a toasty quesadilla. A handheld, cheesy wedge of egg and chopped veggies. This will give you enough energy to set out on any adventure.

SERVES 1

2 large eggs
Hot sauce of your choice
Pinch of kosher salt
1 tablespoon chopped green onions
1 tablespoon finely chopped cilantro
1 teaspoon finely chopped jalapeño
2 teaspoons butter
One 8-inch whole-grain tortilla
½ cup shredded sharp cheddar

For Serving
Sour cream
Salsa

1 In a bowl, whisk the eggs, hot sauce, and salt. Stir in the green onion, cilantro, and jalapeño.

2 Heat an 8-inch skillet over medium heat. Add the butter and cook until it's a light foam, about 1 minute. Pour in your egg mixture and cook until softly scrambled, stirring often, for about 2 minutes. Transfer to a bowl.

3 In a 10-inch skillet, warm a tortilla over medium heat until brown spots appear, for about 45 seconds, then flip. Sprinkle half of the cheese over half of the tortilla. Top the cheese with eggs, then top the eggs with the rest of your cheese.

4 Fold the other half of the tortilla over the toppings. Cook until the bottom is golden brown and crispy, 1 to 2 minutes. Reduce the heat if needed to prevent the tortilla from burning.

5 Flip and cook until golden brown and crispy, another 1 to 2 minutes.

6 Remove the skillet from the heat and transfer the quesadilla to a plate. Cut into quarters.

7 Serve with a side of sour cream and your favorite salsa or hot sauce. Enjoy!

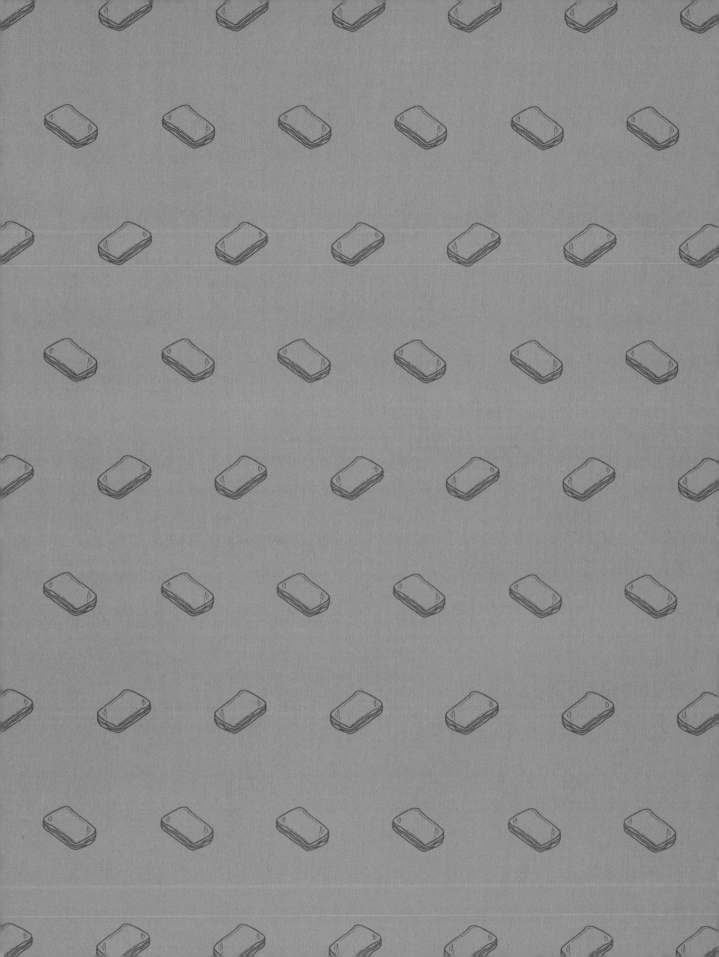

LUNCH

TACO SALAD

This taco salad recipe is basically a family heirloom. Passed down to me from my mother and now to you, buddy. Crush up that bag of tortilla chips with a Paul Coffey 5030 twig, some people's elbows, or a kitchen mallet, and the rest is easy.

SERVES 4

1 pound ground beef
One 1-ounce taco seasoning packet
1 head romaine lettuce, chopped
One 15-ounce can black beans, drained and rinsed
1 cup shredded cheddar
1 cup cherry tomatoes, halved
½ cup thinly sliced black olives
¼ cup thinly sliced green onions
One 8-ounce bottle Catalina salad dressing
One 10-ounce bag Doritos

1 Heat a large skillet over medium-high heat. Add the beef and cook until it's crumbly and no pink is visible, 7 to 8 minutes. Remove from the heat and add ¼ cup of water along with the taco seasoning.

2 Mix together and simmer on low until the water has incorporated and the beef is browned, 5 to 7 minutes. Remove from the heat and let cool.

3 Combine the beef, lettuce, beans, cheddar, tomatoes, olives, and green onions in a large bowl and stir to combine.

4 Add the salad dressing and toss to combine.

5 Crumble the Doritos into bite-size pieces and add them to the bowl. Enjoy!

GRILLED FLUFFERNUTTER

That's a mouthful, eh? Fun to say, fun to make. It's sweet, gooey, and a bit crunchy. Paired best with potato chips and a cold pop, and perfect for sharing with a good buddy. For alternate options, add some bacon, banana, or both.

SERVES 1

¼ cup marshmallow creme, such as Marshmallow Fluff
2 slices whole wheat bread
1 to 2 tablespoons peanut butter
1 tablespoon salted butter

1 Spread the marshmallow creme onto one slice of bread.

2 Spread the peanut butter onto the other slice of bread.

3 Press the two slices of bread together to close the sandwich.

4 Heat a skillet over medium-high heat and add the butter. Add the sandwich and cook until the bread is golden brown and crispy, 2 to 3 minutes on each side.

5 Remove from the skillet. Slice diagonally and enjoy!

CAST-IRON PATTY MELT

A taste of your favorite hole-in-the-wall bar with weeknight karaoke, but save your voice and make this one at home. It's a fusion of a hamburger and grilled cheese sandwich, all in one.

SERVES 4

6 tablespoons (¾ stick) unsalted butter, divided

1 large sweet onion, thinly sliced

1 pound ground beef

8 slices sourdough bread

Kosher salt

Black pepper

4 slices cheddar

4 slices Swiss cheese

Sauce

⅓ cup mayonnaise

2 tablespoons ketchup

½ teaspoon yellow mustard

¼ teaspoon garlic powder

Black pepper

1 Melt 2 tablespoons of butter in a large cast-iron skillet over low heat. Add the onion and cook until soft and golden brown, 25 to 30 minutes, stirring occasionally.

2 Meanwhile, prepare and cook the burger patties.

3 Divide the beef into four sections, then roll into balls. Place one ball between two pieces of parchment paper.

4 Use the flat side of a small unheated skillet to flatten the ball into a thin patty. Remove the parchment paper and season each side with salt and pepper to taste. Repeat with the remaining meat to form four patties.

5 In a medium cast-iron skillet over high heat, cook the patties until the edges start to get crispy, 1 to 2 minutes on one side. Flip and cook until the patties are nicely browned and the edges are crispy, up to 1 minute. Remove from the skillet and set aside.

6 **Make the sauce:** Combine the mayonnaise, ketchup, mustard, garlic powder, and black pepper.

7 Spread a few tablespoons of sauce onto one slice of bread. Top with the onions, burger patty, cheddar, and Swiss cheese, and finish with another piece of bread. Repeat with the remaining ingredients to form four sandwiches.

8 Melt 1 tablespoon of butter in a medium skillet over medium heat. Add one sandwich and cook until crispy and golden on the bottom, about 2 minutes.

9 Remove the sandwich from the pan, then add 1 more tablespoon of butter. Add the sandwich back to the pan, toasted side up, and cook the other side until crispy and golden, 2 minutes. Remove from the skillet, then slice diagonally.

10 Repeat with the remaining butter and sandwiches.

11 Enjoy with any leftover sauce on the side.

CAP'N CRUNCH CHICKEN TENDERS
WITH HONEY MUSTARD GLAZE

One of my favorite cereals makes for the perfect sweet and crispy coating to classic chicken tenders. Fried until golden and crunchy and dipped into honey mustard. Well done, Captain.

SERVES 2

Canola oil
3 cups plain Cap'n Crunch cereal
½ cup all-purpose flour
½ teaspoon onion powder
½ teaspoon garlic powder
1 teaspoon kosher salt, divided
½ teaspoon black pepper
1 large egg
1 pound chicken tenderloins

Honey Mustard Glaze
¼ cup Dijon mustard
3 tablespoons full-fat plain
  Greek yogurt
3 tablespoons local honey, or to taste

1 Pour 1 to 2 inches of canola oil into a large skillet. Heat over medium-high heat to 360°F.

2 Pour the cereal into a large storage bag and use a rolling pin to crush the pieces into crumbs. Pour into a shallow dish.

3 In a second shallow dish, combine the flour, onion powder, garlic powder, ½ teaspoon of salt, and pepper.

4 In a third shallow dish, whisk together the egg and 1 tablespoon of water.

5 Season the chicken tenders with the remaining ½ teaspoon of salt, then dip each tender into the flour mixture to coat.

6 Dip each tender into the egg mixture to coat, then transfer to the dish of crushed cereal and coat completely.

7 **Make the glaze:** In a small bowl, combine the mustard, yogurt, and honey.

8 Place the chicken into the oil and fry until golden brown, about 4 minutes per side.

9 Using a slotted spoon or tongs, remove the tenders from the oil and set on paper towels to drain.

10 Dip into the glaze and enjoy!

GRILLED PESTO
MOZZARELLA SANDWICH

This sandwich used to settle my stomach before big hockey games. Made with slices of fresh tomato, creamy mozzarella cheese, and basil pesto sauce. Placed between two crusty slices of sourdough bread. It's the perfect pregame treat.

SERVES 1

2 tablespoons butter, divided
2 slices sourdough bread
2 tablespoons basil pesto
2 thick slices beefsteak tomato
2 slices fresh mozzarella

1 Place a medium skillet over medium heat. Add 1 tablespoon of butter, then add the bread slices. Cook until golden on the bottom, 2 to 3 minutes, then remove from the skillet.

2 Melt the remaining 1 tablespoon of butter in the skillet, then add the bread back to the pan to brown the other sides, 2 to 3 minutes.

3 Reduce the heat to low and spread the pesto on one side of each slice.

4 Place the mozzarella slices on one slice of bread and top with tomato slices.

5 Place the other slice of bread on top and continue to melt the cheese, 3 minutes.

6 Slice diagonally and enjoy!

BUTTERMILK FRIED CHICKEN SANDWICH

My family's secret recipe, now not so secret anymore. Use this recipe for the crispiest, juiciest chicken sandwich you've ever had. But if it's not—please don't tell my mom.

SERVES 4

2 large chicken breasts
1 cup buttermilk
Canola oil, for frying
2 cups all-purpose flour
1 cup cornstarch
1 tablespoon Cajun seasoning
1 tablespoon onion powder
2 teaspoons garlic powder
2 teaspoons black pepper
1 teaspoon kosher salt
4 brioche buns

For Serving
Beefsteak tomatoes, sliced
Green leaf lettuce
Buttermilk ranch dressing

1 Cut the chicken breasts in half, then place them between two pieces of parchment paper and pound with a mallet to ½-inch thickness.

2 Transfer the chicken to a large sealable bag and add the buttermilk. Place in the fridge to marinate for at least 12 and up to 24 hours, making sure to swish the bag around occasionally.

3 Pour 1 to 2 inches of canola oil into a large skillet. Heat the oil to 360°F.

4 Combine the flour, cornstarch, Cajun seasoning, onion powder, garlic powder, pepper, and salt in a shallow dish.

5 Remove the chicken pieces, one at a time, from the bag and transfer to the dish with the flour mixture. Coat completely on all sides.

6 Place the chicken into the oil and fry until golden brown, about 3 minutes per side.

7 Using a slotted spoon or tongs, remove the tenders from the oil and set on paper towels or a wire rack to cool off.

8 Layer your sandwiches with a drizzle of ranch, fried chicken, a few pieces of lettuce, a thick tomato slice, and another drizzle of ranch. Enjoy!

REUBEN SLIDERS

The perfect gaming snack. I once won the Mushroom Cup in *Mario Kart* while holding one of these sliders.

SERVES 6

One corned beef brisket (about 3 pounds) with seasoning packet

¼ cup Dijon mustard

12 pull-apart Hawaiian rolls

One 16-ounce bottle Thousand Island dressing

2 cups sauerkraut

8 slices Swiss cheese

2 tablespoons melted butter

3 tablespoons chopped fresh parsley

1 Preheat the oven to 350°F. Line a large baking dish with heavy-duty aluminum foil.

2 Rinse the corned beef, then pat dry with paper towels. Place the corned beef, fatty side up, into the baking dish.

3 Top with the mustard, using a brush or rubber spatula to cover all sides of the beef. Sprinkle the corned beef seasoning packet on top. Wrap in the aluminum foil and bake for 1 hour per pound, until the meat is falling apart.

4 Open the foil and set the oven to broil for 5 minutes to crisp the top until golden brown (be careful not to let it burn).

5 Let rest for 5 to 10 minutes. Remove and discard the foil, keeping the brisket and some juices in the baking dish. Shred the meat with two forks.

6 Slice the rolls laterally to create a group of top and bottom buns. Place the bottom halves in another large baking dish.

7 Spread half of the Thousand Island dressing over the whole bottom half of the rolls. Place your desired amount of corned beef on top, followed by the sauerkraut, then the Swiss cheese slices.

8 Top with Thousand Island dressing, then place the top half of the rolls on top. Brush the rolls with melted butter and sprinkle with parsley.

9 Bake for 20 minutes, until the cheese is melted and the buns are toasty.

10 Pull apart the sliders and enjoy!

BACON RANCH PASTA SALAD

Make a couple batches of this pasta salad and stick them in the fridge for a whole week's worth of lunches. This dish is the coolest thing you can bring to a party, next to an acoustic guitar.

SERVES 8 TO 10

1 pound bacon, chopped
Kosher salt
One 12-ounce box rotini
One 15-ounce can peas, drained, or 1½ cups frozen peas
One 10-ounce bag shredded carrots
½ cup mayonnaise
½ cup 2 percent milk
½ cup sour cream
One 1-ounce packet dry ranch seasoning
½ teaspoon garlic powder
1 cup shredded cheddar
1 large tomato, diced
Black pepper

1   Place the bacon pieces in a large skillet and turn the heat to medium. Slowly cook and render the bacon until crispy, about 10 minutes. Drain and set aside.

2   Bring a large pot of salted water to a boil. Add the pasta, peas, and carrots, and cook until the noodles are al dente, about 10 minutes. Drain in a colander and rinse with cold water. Set aside.

3   Whisk together the mayonnaise, milk, sour cream, ranch seasoning, and garlic powder in large bowl.

4   Add the cooled pasta, peas, and carrots, along with the bacon pieces, cheddar, and tomato. Mix well. Season with salt and pepper to taste.

5   Enjoy right away or place in the fridge for 1 to 2 hours to allow the flavors to marinate before serving. Enjoy!

BUFFALO CHICKEN GRILLED CHEESE

This recipe was developed in the Cedar Swamp Lab by combining two childhood favorites: Buffalo wings and grilled cheese. Think lab coats, beakers, and microscopes. A lot of research went into developing the perfect Buffalo chicken grilled cheese sandwich just for you, buddy!

SERVES 2

4 ounces cream cheese, softened
¼ cup crumbled blue cheese
½ teaspoon paprika
¼ teaspoon cayenne
2 cups shredded rotisserie chicken
½ cup hot sauce
½ cup ranch dressing
2 teaspoons minced garlic
4 tablespoons (½ stick) butter
4 slices sourdough bread
4 slices Muenster cheese

1 Combine the cream cheese, blue cheese, paprika, and cayenne in a medium bowl.

2 In another medium bowl, mix the shredded chicken, hot sauce, ranch, and garlic.

3 Butter one side of each of your bread slices. Spread a few tablespoons of the cheese mixture onto the unbuttered side of each slice, then add about ¼ cup of the chicken mixture to each slice. Top each with Muenster cheese, then carefully close the bread to make two sandwiches.

4 Heat a large skillet over medium heat. Add the sandwiches and cook until golden brown, about 4 minutes on each side.

5 Slice diagonally and enjoy!

ALOHA CHEESE SANDWICH

I developed this sandwich in my late twenties while in my Jack Johnson phase. I was in a deep meditative state when I realized that pineapple, although divisive, was the perfect ingredient to create a harmony of flavors with bacon, cheddar cheese, and pizza sauce. Aloha, buddy.

SERVES 1

2 slices sourdough bread
2 tablespoons butter
¼ cup pizza sauce
2 slices Canadian bacon
2 sliced pineapple rings
2 slices cheddar

1   Heat a medium skillet over medium heat. Butter one side of each slice of bread.

2   Place one slice of bread, butter side down, into the skillet and spread with pizza sauce.

3   Top with the Canadian bacon, pineapple rings, and cheddar, then add your other slice of bread, butter side up.

4   Cook until the bread is golden brown and the cheese is melted, about 4 minutes on each side.

5   Slice diagonally and enjoy!

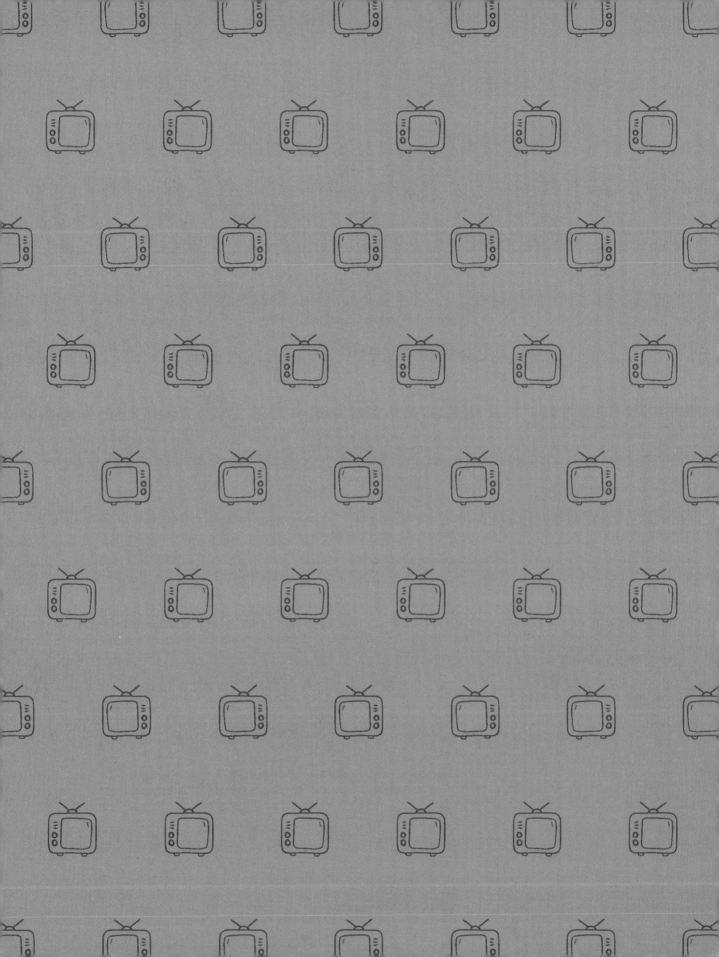

SUPPER

PARMESAN-CRUSTED CHICKEN

Pair this golden cheese-crusted chicken with pasta or veggies and make it a weeknight staple. Every bite is crunchy, cheesy, and juicy, making this recipe one of my personal favorites.

SERVES 4

Nonstick cooking spray
4 large boneless chicken breasts
Kosher salt
Black pepper
½ cup mayonnaise
½ cup freshly grated Parmesan
1 teaspoon Italian seasoning
½ teaspoon garlic powder
Chopped fresh parsley, for serving

1   Preheat the oven to 400°F. Spray a 9 x 13-inch baking dish with cooking spray.

2   Lay the chicken in the dish and season both sides with salt and pepper.

3   In a medium bowl, combine the mayonnaise, Parmesan, Italian seasoning, and garlic powder.

4   Using a spatula, spread the mixture over top of the chicken breasts to cover completely.

5   Bake the chicken for 20 to 25 minutes, until the chicken reaches an internal temperature of 165°F and there is a nicely browned crust on top.

6   Let the chicken rest for 5 minutes. Top with chopped parsley and enjoy!

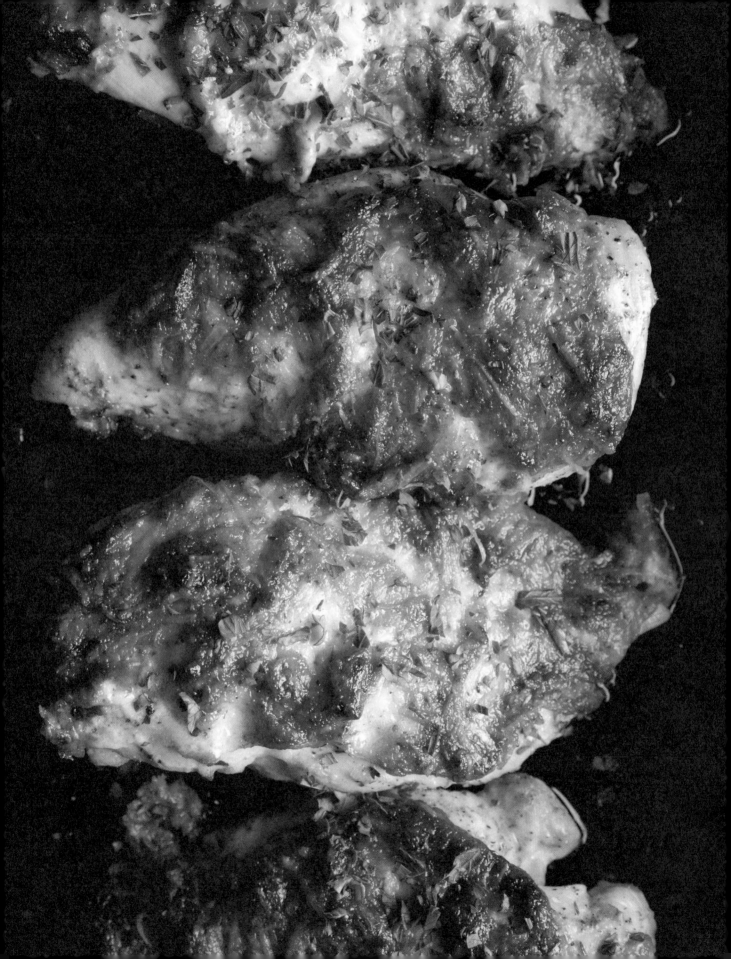

Here's what's cooking: Potato Casserole

Recipe from the kitchen of:

2 # hash brown potatoes thawed
1 stick margerine melted
1 can crm chx soup
____ cup chopped onions or more
____ salt ___ 16 oz cheddar chee

HASH BROWN POTATO CASSEROLE

Feed all the cousins with this old family recipe. I hope this casserole creates as many memories for your family as it has for mine. The crispy corn flake topping with the cheesy potatoes below are the greatest team since the 2001–2002 Detroit Red Wings.

SERVES 6 TO 8

Nonstick cooking spray
One 30-ounce bag frozen shredded
  hash browns, thawed
One 10.5-ounce can cream of
  chicken soup
1 cup shredded cheddar
1 cup sour cream
½ cup chopped onion
1½ teaspoons kosher salt
½ cup (1 stick) melted butter
1 cup corn flakes cereal

1 Preheat the oven to 325°F. Spray a 9 x 13-inch baking dish with cooking spray.

2 In a large bowl, combine the hash browns, cream of chicken soup, cheddar, sour cream, onion, and salt. Mix well, then transfer to the baking dish

3 Top the mixture with the corn flakes and evenly pour the melted margarine over top.

4 Bake for 1½ hours, until the mixture is bubbly and the corn flakes are golden brown and crispy. Enjoy!

MOM'S STUFFED CABBAGE

This is a generational recipe handed down from my great-grandmother. I can still picture my mom in the kitchen with an ice cream scooper, placing the mixture into the cabbage leaves—which is both a beautiful memory and an expert tip for this recipe!

SERVES 3

Nonstick cooking spray
1 large head of cabbage, leaves separated
1 pound ground beef
1 cup cooked white rice
¼ cup chopped onion
1 egg, beaten
Kosher salt
Black pepper
One 10.75-ounce can tomato soup
2 cups sauerkraut

1 Preheat the oven to 350°F. Spray a 9-inch square baking dish with cooking spray.

2 Bring a large pot of water to a boil. Add the cabbage leaves and blanch until wilted and soft, 1 minute. Transfer the leaves to paper towels to drain.

3 In a medium skillet over medium-high heat, cook the beef until browned, crumbly, and no longer pink, 5 to 7 minutes. Drain.

4 In a large bowl, combine the beef, rice, onion, egg, and salt and pepper to taste. Mix well.

5 Set out your cabbage leaves and spoon about ¼ cup of the beef mixture into each leaf.

6 Roll up the leaves, encasing the beef mixture, being careful to tuck in the ends.

7 Place the cabbage rolls, seam side down, into the baking dish. Pour the soup over the rolls, then top with sauerkraut.

8 Cover with foil and bake for 90 minutes, until the soup is bubbly. Enjoy!

TACO SHELL CUPS

Tired of the same old taco night, eh? Switch it up with these taco cups. Utilize a muffin tin to craft tortilla cups to hold all your favorite taco ingredients. Eat with a fork or just take a big bite.

SERVES 4 TO 6

Nonstick cooking spray
12 small flour tortillas
6 ounces shredded rotisserie chicken
One 15-ounce can black beans, drained
1 cup shredded cheddar
1 cup salsa
1 teaspoon garlic powder
½ teaspoon ground cumin
1 cup shredded lettuce
1 cup sour cream
1 jalapeño, thinly sliced

1 Preheat the oven to 350°F. Spray a 12-cup muffin pan with cooking spray.

2 Warm the tortillas in the microwave until they're pliable, about 20 seconds. Push the tortillas down into the cups to make bowls, making sure to press into the edges to form a flat bottom.

3 Bake for 10 minutes, until the tortillas are slightly crisp and starting to brown. Remove from the oven, keeping the tortillas in the pan to let cool.

4 While the tortilla bowls are in the oven, make the chicken mixture. In a medium bowl, combine the chicken, beans, cheddar, salsa, garlic powder, and cumin.

5 Fill each tortilla bowl with the chicken mixture, then return to the oven for 10 minutes, until the cheese is melted.

6 Remove from the oven and top each bowl with shredded lettuce, sour cream, and sliced jalapeño.

7 Carefully lift the bowls from the pan and enjoy!

CHICKEN POT PIE CASSEROLE

Warm chicken and a medley of veggies are tucked in together under a crisp, buttery biscuit crust, like a cozy bed on a cold day. This recipe has been a comfort food for me since I was a kid, coming inside after a long day of playing in the snow.

SERVES 6

Nonstick cooking spray
2 cups shredded chicken
One 10.5-ounce can cream of
  chicken soup
1½ cups frozen mixed veggies
1 cup cheddar
1 cup sour cream
1 teaspoon kosher salt
1 teaspoon garlic powder
One 16.3-ounce can biscuit dough

1 Preheat the oven to 375°F. Spray a 9-inch square baking dish with cooking spray.

2 In a large bowl, mix the chicken, soup, veggies, cheddar, sour cream, salt, and garlic powder. Mix well, then pour the mixture into the baking dish.

3 Separate the biscuits and cut each one into fourths, then place them on top of the chicken mixture.

4 Bake for 35 to 45 minutes, until the biscuits are golden brown and the casserole is bubbling (see Tip). Enjoy!

Tip: If the biscuits start to brown too much before they are cooked through, cover the baking dish with foil and continue to cook.

BUSY DAY SOUP

We've all been there, buddy. Just as it's titled, make this soup when you've had a busy day. When you're ready to call it a night, the smell of this soup will call you into the kitchen as it simmers. Let the worries of the day just drift away.

SERVES 4

1 pound ground beef
Kosher salt
Black pepper
One 1-ounce packet onion soup mix
One 28-ounce can diced tomatoes
1¾ cups frozen mixed veggies
1 cup macaroni

1 Cook the beef in a large soup pot over medium-high heat until it's crumbly and no pink remains, 5 to 7 minutes. Drain the fat, then season to taste with salt and pepper.

2 Add 5 cups of water, the onion soup mix, and the diced tomatoes and stir to combine.

3 Simmer over medium heat for about 30 minutes.

4 Add the veggies and macaroni to the pot and simmer for 10 to 15 more minutes, until the macaroni is al dente. Season to taste and enjoy!

PARMESAN BAKED PORK CHOPS

My favorite way to have pork chops. This recipe is as easy as falling off a log and makes for a great last-minute dinner idea.

SERVES 4

4 boneless pork chops, ½ inch thick
1 tablespoon olive oil
Kosher salt
Black pepper
1 cup Italian bread crumbs
1 cup shredded Parmesan
1 teaspoon garlic powder

1. Preheat the oven to 350°F. Place a wire rack onto a baking sheet.

2. Rub the pork chops with olive oil. Season both sides with salt and pepper.

3. In a shallow dish, mix the bread crumbs, Parmesan, 1 teaspoon pepper, and garlic powder.

4. Press the pork chops into the breading mixture, coating on all sides. Place the pork chops onto the wire rack.

5. Bake for 25 to 35 minutes, until the internal temperature reaches 145°F and the bread crumbs are toasted.

6. Let rest for 7 to 10 minutes so the pork remains juicy. Enjoy!

LOADED BAKED POTATO SOUP

Grab a hard hat, a lunch pail, and a potato masher for this one, buddy. This soup is made with Idaho potatoes, a creamy, cheesy base, and crispy, crumbled bacon to top it off. Spoil yourself with this soup, a movie marathon, and a cozy night in.

SERVES 6

4 large Idaho potatoes
10 strips bacon, chopped
10 tablespoons butter
$\frac{2}{3}$ cup all-purpose flour
2 teaspoons kosher salt
¼ teaspoon black pepper
6 cups 2 percent milk
1 cup sour cream
1 cup shredded cheddar
¼ cup thinly sliced green onions

1 Preheat the oven to 400°F.

2 Poke the potatoes all over with a fork, then transfer to a baking sheet and bake for 1 hour, until soft and cooked through. Let cool enough to handle, then remove the skins.

3 While the potatoes are baking, cook your bacon. Add the bacon to a large skillet and cook over medium heat until crispy, 8 to 10 minutes. Remove and transfer to a paper towel to drain.

4 In a large soup pot, melt the butter over medium-high heat.

5 Stir in the flour, salt, and pepper and let cook for about 2 minutes, stirring constantly to make a roux. Gradually whisk in the milk, then bring to a boil. Continue to stir until thickened, about 2 minutes.

6 Add the potatoes to the pot. Using a potato masher, mash the potatoes until the soup thickens. Some chunks are okay.

7 Remove from the heat, then stir in the sour cream. Serve with cheese, green onions, and bacon on top. Enjoy!

LEMON CHICKEN
WITH PENNE & ASPARAGUS

Grab one of your best skillets for this dish. Lemon really brightens up the chicken, and when paired with buttery asparagus and creamy penne, it makes for the perfect blueprint to a successful supper.

SERVES 3 TO 4

1 pound boneless chicken breast, cut into 1-inch cubes

Kosher salt

Black pepper

2 tablespoons olive oil

2 tablespoons butter

3 garlic cloves, minced

One 14.5-ounce can chicken broth (1½ cups)

10 ounces penne

1 pound asparagus, ends trimmed

4 ounces cream cheese, softened

½ cup shredded Parmesan

Zest and juice of 1 large lemon

Lemon wedges, for serving

1 Season the chicken with salt and pepper.

2 Heat the oil in a large, deep skillet over medium-high heat.

3 Add the chicken and cook until golden brown, about 8 minutes, turning the pieces halfway through cooking. Remove the chicken from the skillet and set aside.

4 Add the butter and garlic to the skillet and cook over medium heat until the garlic is fragrant, about 30 seconds. Add the chicken broth and 1½ cups of water and bring to a boil.

5 Add the penne, then cover and boil until al dente, 8 minutes.

6 Cut the asparagus into 1-inch pieces and add them to the skillet. Cover and cook until the asparagus is cooked through and tender-crisp, 3 to 4 minutes.

7 Add the cream cheese, Parmesan, lemon zest, and lemon juice. Stir to combine.

8 Add the chicken, then remove from the heat. Serve with lemon wedges and enjoy!

SLOPPY JOE STICKS

A staple of pond hockey season in my snowy northern Michigan town, this dish was the only way my mom could get us off the ice when I was a kid. It's a twist on a classic childhood recipe that can feed the whole team.

SERVES 4

½ medium yellow onion, diced
2 to 3 tablespoons butter, divided
1 pound ground beef
1 teaspoon garlic powder
1 teaspoon Italian seasoning
Kosher salt
Black pepper
One 15-ounce can thick Sloppy Joe sauce
1 loaf of French bread, split open
3 cups shredded cheddar

1 Preheat the oven to 350°F. Line a baking sheet with parchment paper.

2 To a large skillet over medium-high heat, add the onion and 1 tablespoon of butter. Cook until the onions are soft, 5 to 6 minutes.

3 Add the beef and season with garlic powder, Italian seasoning, and salt and pepper to your preference. Cook until crumbly and no pink remains, 7 to 8 minutes.

4 Drain the grease, then add the Sloppy Joe sauce. Simmer until warmed through, about 2 minutes.

5 Butter each half of the bread with the remaining butter, then place on the baking sheet.

6 Spread the Sloppy Joe mixture onto the bread and cover with cheese.

7 Bake for 10 to 15 minutes, until the bread is toasted and cheese is melty.

8 Slice into breadsticks and enjoy!

SLOW COOKER

FIESTA CORN DIP

Whether you have company in town or your parents are out of town, this fiesta dip was made for parties. So get a healthy scoop of this colorful dip and break out the salsa hips, buddy. For a casual gathering, game night, or festive celebration, this dip will be your new go-to appetizer. Serve with tortilla chips, vegetable sticks, crackers, or pita bread.

SERVES 6

Three 15-ounce cans of corn, drained
One 14.5-ounce can diced tomatoes with green chiles
8 ounces cream cheese, softened
2 cups shredded pepper jack
1 green bell pepper, diced
½ cup sour cream
1 jalapeño, diced
1½ teaspoons kosher salt
½ teaspoon chili powder
Tortilla chips or Fritos, for serving

1 Add the corn, tomatoes and green chiles, cream cheese, pepper jack, bell pepper, sour cream, jalapeño, salt, and chili powder to a slow cooker. Mix well.

2 Cook on high for 2 hours, stirring intermittently, until the cheese is melted and the veggies are softened.

3 Serve with tortilla chips or Fritos on the side. Enjoy!

PINEAPPLE CHICKEN

This sweet chicken dish is simple and will last you a couple suppers. Tender chicken cooked in sweet pineapple juice, brown sugar, and soy sauce. Best served on a warmed Hawaiian roll, aside steamed veggies, or atop coconut rice.

SERVES 4

2 pounds chicken tenderloins
1 cup pineapple juice
½ cup dark brown sugar
⅓ cup soy sauce

1 Add all of the ingredients to a slow cooker.

2 Cook on low for 7 hours, until tender. Shred and enjoy!

BANANA FRENCH TOAST

Picture this, buddy: It's a special morning with your loved ones. Everyone gathers in amazement around your slow cooker, which beautifully displays slices of day-old baguette, topped with tree juice, pecans, and bananas. It's believed that it was this French toast recipe, and not his uncanny work ethic, that won my grandfather his Christmas bonus in 1982.

SERVES 6

Nonstick cooking spray
1 day-old baguette
8 ounces cream cheese, softened
3 eggs
1½ cups whole milk
¼ cup light brown sugar
½ tablespoon vanilla extract
1 teaspoon ground cinnamon
1 teaspoon ground nutmeg
2 bananas
2 tablespoons butter, thinly sliced

For Serving
Banana slices
½ cup chopped pecans
Grade A tree juice (maple syrup)

1 Spray a slow cooker with cooking spray. Cut the baguette crosswise into 1-inch slices.

2 Spread the cream cheese over both sides of each baguette slice and place at the bottom of the slow cooker.

3 In a large bowl, beat the eggs, then add in your milk, sugar, vanilla, cinnamon, and nutmeg. Mash the bananas into the mixture with a whisk until well combined.

4 Pour the mixture over top of the bread slices and press the bread down into the mixture so it soaks up a lot of the liquid. Let sit for at least 30 minutes.

5 Place the butter slices on top of the bread.

6 Cook on low for 3½ hours, until the egg mixture has fully set.

7 Serve with banana slices, pecans, and tree juice. Enjoy!

CHICKEN DUMPLING SOUP

Battle a chilly brisk day with this chicken dumpling soup. The warm broth, tender chicken, and pillowy dumplings create a bed of comfort with every bite. The biscuits make for a hearty addition to this creamy and delicious soup. As you wait, watch one of your favorite films. You'll want to enjoy this under a warm blanket, with a good book.

SERVES 7 TO 8

Nonstick cooking spray
1 pound boneless chicken breast
Kosher salt
Black pepper
2 cups chicken broth
1 teaspoon Italian seasoning
½ teaspoon dried thyme
5 carrots, peeled and sliced into
   ½-inch rounds
4 celery stalks, cut into ½-inch pieces
1 large sweet onion, diced
2 garlic cloves, minced
2 tablespoons butter, sliced
One 10.5-ounce can cream of
   mushroom soup
One 10.5-ounce can cream of
   chicken soup
One 10-ounce can biscuit dough

1 Spray a slow cooker with cooking spray.

2 Salt and pepper the chicken and add to the bottom of the slow cooker.

3 Pour in the chicken broth and add the Italian seasoning and thyme. Stir to combine. Add the carrots and celery, then stir in the onion and garlic.

4 Add the butter, then pour the cream of mushroom and cream of chicken soup over top.

5 Cook on low for 7 hours, until the ingredients are fully incorporated and the chicken is ready to shred. Remove the chicken, shred, and return to the pot.

6 Cut each biscuit into quarters and drop them into the slow cooker over top of the soup.

7 Cook on high for an additional hour, until the biscuits are fully cooked. Enjoy!

BEEF CHILI

This six-can chili is a heavyweight contender in any chili cook-off. I once made it at a Detroit Lions vs. Dallas Cowboys tailgate in 2013, and it made a man in a cowboy hat's eyes light up like stars in the night sky. Simmer on high for at least four hours, or until the beans are as "soft as a prairie sunset"—Guy in cowboy hat, 2013.

SERVES 8

1 pound ground beef
Kosher salt
Black pepper
Two 10.75-ounce cans tomato soup
One 14.5-ounce can diced tomatoes
  with green chiles
One 14.75-ounce can creamed corn
One 15-ounce can black beans
One 15-ounce can red kidney beans
1 jalapeño, sliced

For Serving
Sour cream
1 cup shredded cheddar

1   In a large skillet over medium-high heat, cook the ground beef until crumbly and no longer pink, 5 minutes. Season with salt and pepper.

2   Transfer the beef, with all of the fat, into the slow cooker.

3   Add the tomato soup, diced tomatoes and green chiles, corn, black beans, and kidney beans, plus any canning liquid. Add half of the jalapeño, 1 teaspoon of salt, and ½ teaspoon of pepper to the slow cooker.

4   Cook on high for 4 hours.

5   Top with sour cream, cheese, and remaining jalapeño. Enjoy!

CHEESY SAUSAGE DIP

Dipping into this creamy, hearty dish is like a savory treasure hunt. And the medallions of sausage, sprinkled amongst the cheesy potatoes, are the gold. Use a thick slice of baguette as your shovel and dive in.

SERVES 10 TO 12

14 ounces smoked beef sausage, diced
½ cup diced yellow onion
One 30-ounce bag frozen shredded hash browns, thawed
One 10.5-ounce can cream of celery soup
One 8-ounce container French onion dip
One 8-ounce container sour cream
2 cups shredded cheddar, divided
¼ teaspoon Old Bay seasoning
⅛ teaspoon black pepper
Nonstick cooking spray

For Serving
Sliced, toasted baguette
Tortilla chips
Fritos scoops

1   Add the sausage and onion to a large skillet over high heat and cook until the onion is translucent and the sausage has browned, about 5 minutes.

2   In a large bowl, combine the hash browns, cream of celery soup, French onion dip, sour cream, 1¾ cups of cheddar, the Old Bay, and pepper.

3   Coat the slow cooker with cooking spray, then add half of the hash brown mixture.

4   Add in the sausage and onion, then add the other half of the hash brown mixture and top with the remaining ¼ cup of cheddar.

5   Cook on low for 3 hours, until the cheese is melted and bubbly. Enjoy with toasted baguette, tortilla chips, or Fritos scoops!

CHICKEN TORTILLA SOUP

A torn, stained, and folded note card holds this old family recipe. It might be old, but it's still used on the regular in the Cedar Swamp. Everything you love about chicken tacos is made into a spicy, creamy soup, topped with crunchy tortilla pieces. The mix of creamy and crunchy textures makes this soup a strong taco night contender.

SERVES 5

1 pound boneless chicken breast
Kosher salt
Black pepper
1 medium yellow onion, chopped
2 garlic cloves, minced
One 15-ounce can corn
One 14.5-ounce can diced tomatoes
   with green chiles
One 10-ounce can enchilada sauce
3 cups chicken broth
One 1-ounce packet taco seasoning
½ teaspoon chili powder
One 15-ounce can black beans,
   drained

For Serving
Tortilla chips
Shredded cheddar

1   Place the chicken in the slow cooker and season with salt and pepper. Add the onion and garlic.

2   Add the corn, and tomatoes with green chiles, plus any canning liquid from the corn and tomatoes. Add the enchilada sauce.

3   Pour in the chicken broth, then mix in the taco seasoning and chili powder.

4   Cook on low for 9 hours, until the chicken is ready to shred and all of the flavors have incorporated.

5   Remove the chicken, shred, and return to the slow cooker along with the beans to cook on low for an additional 15 minutes, until everything is heated through.

6   Crumble your desired amount of tortilla chips, then sprinkle the chips and shredded cheddar on top. Enjoy!

HEARTY POTATOES & KIELBASA

Let the slow cooker work its magic as it nurtures the kielbasa, potatoes, and cabbage into soft and savory goodness. This is the best meal to have waiting for you when you get home from a long day. A well-prepared meal without any immediate effort is a comforting win I'll gladly devour.

SERVES 5

1 tablespoon olive oil

12 ounces kielbasa, sliced into ½-inch pieces

5 medium russet potatoes, peeled and diced

1 small head green cabbage, chopped into 2-inch pieces

1½ cups chicken broth

1 white onion, sliced

1 teaspoon dried parsley

1 teaspoon dried thyme

½ teaspoon kosher salt

¼ teaspoon black pepper

⅛ teaspoon cayenne

1 Heat the olive oil in a large skillet over medium heat. Add the kielbasa and cook until browned, about 5 minutes. Transfer to the slow cooker.

2 Add the potatoes, cabbage, and onion. Cover with chicken broth, then add the parsley, thyme, salt, pepper, and cayenne. Mix well.

3 Cook on low for 3 to 4 hours, until the sausage, cabbage, and potatoes are tender. Enjoy!

SLOW COOKER
BAKED SWEET POTATOES

It was always a treat to smell the familiar aroma of sweet potatoes and cinnamon coming from the kitchen. This simple weeknight dish almost feels like dessert. The potatoes have a creamy, earthy, melt-in-your-mouth sensation that leaves you more than satisfied.

SERVES 3 TO 4

5 medium sweet potatoes
5 tablespoons butter
5 to 10 tablespoons dark brown sugar
$5/8$ teaspoon ground cinnamon

1   Use a fork to poke holes all over the sweet potatoes.

2   Cut off a large square of aluminum foil and place a $1/2$-tablespoon slice of butter in the center. Set one sweet potato on top of the butter.

3   Place another $1/2$-tablespoon slice of butter on top of the sweet potato. Sprinkle in 1 to 2 tablespoons of brown sugar and $1/8$ teaspoon of cinnamon. Close up the foil, encasing the sweet potato fully.

4   Repeat with the remaining sweet potatoes, butter, sugar, and cinnamon.

5   Place the wrapped sweet potatoes in the slow cooker, seam side up so the butter doesn't leak out.

6   Cook on low for 4 to 5 hours until the sweet potatoes are soft, not firm.

7   Remove the potatoes with tongs, then unwrap and slice down the middle. Gently fluff up some of the sweet potato with a fork.

8   Pour the melted butter, cinnamon, and brown sugar mixture from the foil over the sweet potato. Enjoy!

WHITE CHICKEN CHILI

Let this white chicken chili cook itself while you enjoy some time to unwind, buddy! Sit back, relax, and enjoy the aroma as a neighborhood of new flavors mingle and simmer. There is joy in sharing a good pot of chili, but if you want to savor the fruits of your labor alone, ensure the coast is clear, lock the doors, and close the windows. Some meals are just too good to share!

SERVES 3

1 pound boneless chicken breast
1 teaspoon ground cumin
½ teaspoon chili powder
¼ teaspoon cayenne
Kosher salt
Black pepper
1 yellow onion, chopped
2 garlic cloves, minced
Two 15-ounce cans great northern
  beans, drained
One 15-ounce can corn, drained
Two 4-ounce cans chopped
  green chiles
3 cups chicken broth
4 ounces cream cheese, softened
¼ cup half and half

1   Place the chicken in the slow cooker and season with the cumin, chili powder, cayenne, salt, and pepper. Add the onion and garlic.

2   Add the beans, corn and green chiles, then pour the chicken broth over everything.

3   Cook on low for 8 hours.

4   Remove the chicken to shred, then return to the slow cooker.

5   Add the cream cheese and half and half and cook on high for an additional 15 minutes, until the cream cheese is fully incorporated.

6   Stir well and enjoy!

CAMPFIRE

Recently, I stumbled upon an old hollow log, and what time has forgotten, the eldest black bear and I remember fondly. This log was a feeding trough, carved from northern white cedar by my grandfather's hands. It was brought here through a field of flooded timber, through wild mint and watercress, past where the birch trees hold hands, into a second-growth pine forest, and to this exact spot over thirty years ago. It was once a vessel of life, nourishing the whitetail deer, porcupines, squirrels, chipmunks, black bears, and turkeys that call the farthest corners of our Cedar Swamp home. A cedar tree, which once was just a small cone carried by the wind and fed by the sun, sprouted into a sapling—a sapling that would grow to be well over fifty feet tall. And what once fed the entire forest is now a quilt of moss, pine needles, and maple leaves, slowly returning to the same earth from which it sprung.

Nearby, about thirty-seven yards southwest, beneath the same canopy of chirping birds and tall white pines, lies a small campfire pit made from eleven rocks arranged in a circle. Each rock, unique in shape and size, was placed here by my grandfather sometime in the early 1990s. This campfire pit is the same one where I have cooked many times—in front of bluebirds, blue jays, carpenter ants, red squirrels, mink frogs, chipmunks, and red-bellied snakes, and in front of millions of people around the world on social media apps like TikTok, Instagram, and YouTube. Like the feeding trough, this campsite is a vessel of life, too, holding many cherished memories shared over a good meal.

These locations bring forth profound joy, the kind that only campfire cooking can inspire.

Here, if I listen closely, I can still hear my grandfather's voice asking me to gather more sticks—to add to the dwindling pile I had collected just minutes before—or hear him explaining how to make the perfect grilled cheese by keeping an even fire and cooking it low and slow, using water and a cover to steam the cheese and bread to perfection. But my favorite feeling that campfire cooking brings is the warmth of an open flame, contested by a cold, dark, starry sky. A fire, built by hand and fueled by the elements, makes even my Cold Pop Chocolate Caramel Lava Cake (on page 140) taste better than ever. When paired with the relaxing sound of a creek, the chirping of birds, and maybe even some *NHL 96* on Game Boy, it doesn't get much better.

Whether you're cooking for a crowd or cooking solo, playing classic Game Boy or listening to the birds sing, when you cook outside over a campfire, you're never alone. The unseen world thrives right beside us, and with it comes an invisible camaraderie—the same camaraderie that I like to think our ancestors felt, gathered under the stars or in a dark cave, around an open fire, enjoying a good story and maybe a pot of hot goulash. Cooking in the open air inspires us to get back to basics, while also thinking a little bit outside the box. Whether you're grilling, barbecuing, or cooking over a campfire, it's a chance to reconnect with nature on a deep and fundamental level. Basic enamel pots and pans, camp utensils, and wooden plates remind us that we don't need much to enjoy a good meal. But, to enjoy a great meal, I suggest cooking it in nature, over a fire and under the open sky, inside eleven rocks.

CAST-IRON SKILLET

SHRIMP FAJITAS

Make sure you're ready to make enough of these shrimp fajitas for the whole camp. Neighboring noses will be sure to stop over for a bite. These fajitas spare no dramatics as they sizzle and smell amazing while roasting over the fire.

SERVES 6

1 teaspoon chili powder
1 teaspoon ground cumin
½ teaspoon garlic powder
½ teaspoon onion powder
½ teaspoon smoked paprika
1 pound large shrimp, peeled and deveined, tails removed
1 tablespoon olive oil
1 green bell pepper, thinly sliced
1 red bell pepper, thinly sliced
1 yellow bell pepper, thinly sliced
1 small white or red onion, thinly sliced
Kosher salt
Black pepper

For Serving
Flour or corn tortillas
Shredded Mexican blend cheese
Sour cream
Guacamole
Fresh cilantro
Lime wedges

1 In a medium bowl, mix the chili powder, cumin, garlic powder, onion powder, and paprika. Add the shrimp and toss to coat.

2 In a large cast-iron skillet over the fire, heat the olive oil over high heat.

3 Add the bell peppers and onion to the skillet and cook until tender and soft, 4 to 5 minutes. Season with salt and pepper, then remove from the skillet.

4 Add the shrimp to the skillet and cook until pink and opaque, 2 to 3 minutes per side. Reintroduce the veggies to the skillet.

5 Serve in warm tortillas with your favorite toppings. Mine are guacamole, shredded cheese, cilantro, sour cream, and fresh squeezed lime wedges. Enjoy!

SKILLET CORNBREAD

This cornbread could steal the show if you made it as a companion dish. Sop up some of our six-can chili (on page 94) with a chunk of this cornbread and thank me later. If enjoying on its own, top with butter and a drizzle of honey.

SERVES 8

4 tablespoons (½ stick) butter
3 tablespoons honey
2 eggs
1 cup milk
1 cup cornmeal
½ cup all-purpose flour
1 tablespoon baking powder
½ teaspoon kosher salt

1   In a 10-inch cast-iron skillet, melt the butter over medium-high heat, then remove from the fire.

2   In a large bowl, mix the honey and eggs until smooth. Mix in the milk and half of the melted butter.

3   Add in the cornmeal, flour, baking powder, and salt. Mix well.

4   Set the skillet over medium-low heat to rewarm the remaining butter in the skillet and coat the bottom. Pour in the batter, making an even layer.

5   Cover the skillet with foil and make slits in the top to allow for ventilation.

6   Cook for 15 to 20 minutes. Remove from the heat and let the covered cornbread rest for an additional 5 minutes, until it starts to pull away slightly from the edges of the pan. Enjoy!

LOADED SMASH POTATOES

Listen to the wind blow, the birds call, and the sizzling sound of potatoes hitting the skillet. These savory potato bites are a great midday snack for your fellow campers. The skillet gives them their crisp edges while maintaining a soft interior, resulting in a melt-in-your-mouth treat.

SERVES 3 TO 4

1 pound fingerling potatoes
3 slices bacon, chopped
Kosher salt
Black pepper
1 cup shredded cheddar
Sour cream
1 tablespoon chopped chives

1 Fill a large pot with water and bring to a boil. Add the potatoes and cook until fork-tender, 12 to 15 minutes. Drain and set aside.

2 Meanwhile, in a large skillet over medium-low heat, fry the bacon until crispy, 7 to 8 minutes. Remove the bacon and set on a paper towel–lined plate. Leave a thin layer of bacon grease in the skillet.

3 Use the bottom of a cup or a large spoon to gently press down and smash each potato until they are ½-inch thick.

4 Heat the skillet over medium-high heat, then add the smashed potatoes. Season with salt and pepper.

5 Cook until crispy on the bottom, 3 to 4 minutes. Using a spatula, flip the potatoes and cook until crispy on the other side, 3 to 4 more minutes.

6 Add the cheese, then remove from the fire.

7 Drizzle with sour cream, sprinkle with bacon, and top with chives. Enjoy!

COWBOY BREAKFAST

Fuel your cowboy spirit and wake up early to make this picture-perfect breakfast, which is sure to impress your fellow campers. This skillet is packed with eggs, bacon, potatoes, and spices—plenty to keep you energized throughout a long day in nature.

SERVES 3

4 slices bacon

One 30-ounce bag frozen shredded hash browns, thawed

⅛ teaspoon garlic powder

⅛ teaspoon onion powder

Kosher salt

Black pepper

1 cup shredded cheddar, divided

6 eggs, whisked

Sliced scallions, for serving

1   Place a large skillet over medium-high heat. Add the bacon and cook until crispy, about 10 minutes. Transfer the bacon to a paper towel–lined plate, leaving the grease in the pan.

2   Add the hash browns to the skillet. Sprinkle with garlic powder, onion powder and a dash of salt and pepper. Cook the potatoes until golden and crispy, 12 to 15 minutes, stirring occasionally.

3   Sprinkle ¾ cup cheese on top of the hash browns.

4   Pour the whisked eggs over top.

5   Crumble the bacon and sprinkle over top. Add the remaining shredded cheese.

6   Cook until the eggs have set, 15 to 20 minutes. Garnish with sliced scallions and enjoy!

SKILLET FRENCH TOAST
WITH STRAWBERRIES

Ripped chunks of croissant make this recipe unique and next level. Paired with fresh strawberries and preserves, this French toast is sure to impress all your buddies.

SERVES 8 TO 10

8 eggs
3 cups whole milk
¼ cup grade A tree juice
  (maple syrup)
1 tablespoon pure vanilla extract
¼ teaspoon kosher salt
1 cup strawberry preserves
8 croissants, torn into chunks
2 cups strawberries, trimmed
  and quartered
½ cup chopped pecans
Powdered sugar, for dusting

1 Whisk the eggs in a large bowl, then whisk in the milk, tree juice, vanilla, and salt until frothy.

2 Pour the strawberry preserves into a small saucepan over low heat and heat through.

3 Place half of the croissant chunks in the bottom of a large cast-iron skillet. Pour half of the warm preserves over top, then pour in half of the egg mixture.

4 Repeat the process again with another layer of croissant, preserves, and egg. Gently press down and let sit for 30 minutes to allow the croissants to soak up the mixture.

5 Sprinkle with fresh strawberries and pecans, then cover the skillet with aluminum foil.

6 Bake for 30 minutes, then remove the aluminum foil and continue cooking for 15 minutes or until golden brown.

7 Dust with powdered sugar before serving and enjoy!

MONKEY BREAD

A classic Boy Scout recipe and one of the first things I ever cooked over the fire. I can remember how intimidating campfire cooking was, but this classic recipe is a perfect example of how easy and delicious it actually can be. I later adapted this monkey bread into a foil pack version (on page 174).

SERVES 6 TO 8

½ cup granulated sugar
2 teaspoons ground cinnamon
One 16.3-ounce can flaky biscuit
    dough
12 tablespoons (1½ sticks) butter
1 cup brown sugar
¼ cup pecan pieces, toasted

1 In a large bowl, mix the granulated sugar and cinnamon.

2 Separate the biscuits on a cutting board. Cut each biscuit into six pieces.

3 Place a medium skillet over medium heat. Add the butter and heat until melted. Stir in the brown sugar. Remove from the heat and set aside.

4 Pour half of the melted butter mixture into the bowl with the cinnamon sugar.

5 Place a large skillet over medium high heat.

6 Toss each biscuit piece in the cinammon sugar, then place onto the skillet, making a single layer.

7 Pour the other half of the brown sugar–butter mixture over top of the biscuits.

8 Cook until the biscuits have risen, about 25 minutes.

9 Remove from the heat and sprinkle with pecans. Enjoy!

CHEESY PEPPERONI ROLLS

These rolls are fun to make and always rise to perfection over the fire. When paired with marinara, they taste even better than your typical late-night pizza run. Don't forget the melted butter and Parmesan cheese to finish.

MAKES 12 ROLLS

All-purpose flour
1 pound pizza dough
½ cup marinara sauce
¼ cup freshly grated Parmesan, plus more for topping
1 cup freshly shredded mozzarella, plus more for topping
1 cup sliced pepperoni
1 green bell pepper, chopped
1½ teaspoons dried oregano
½ teaspoon red pepper flakes
¼ cup chopped fresh basil
Olive oil
1 tablespoon butter
½ teaspoon garlic salt
Chopped fresh parsley, for serving

1 Dust a large cutting board with flour and roll out your pizza dough into a large rectangle, about ¼-inch thick.

2 Spread the pizza sauce over the dough, leaving about ½ inch of space to the top edge.

3 Evenly distribute the Parmesan, mozzarella, pepperoni, bell pepper, oregano, red pepper flakes, and basil.

4 Starting with the edge closest to you, roll the pizza dough into a long log. Pinch the ends and press the edges of the dough together to seal it up. Use a sharp serrated knife to cut into 1½-inch slices, making your pizza rolls.

5 Rub a large skillet evenly with olive oil. Place the pinwheels into the skillet in an even layer and cover with a hand towel. Let the dough rise for 30 minutes.

6 Get the fire ready to cook over medium-high heat. Place the skillet over the fire and cook until the dough is just starting to brown and the cheese is melted, about 20 minutes. Remove from the heat.

7 Place a small skillet over the fire and melt the butter, 1 to 2 minutes. Stir in the garlic salt, then remove from the fire.

8 Brush the pizza rolls with melted butter and sprinkle with extra Parmesan and mozzarella.

9 Return the large skillet to the fire and cook the pizza rolls until golden, 5 to 10 minutes.

10 Sprinkle with chopped parsley and enjoy!

BREADED CHICKEN PARMESAN

A main dish that will impress at the fire and elevate the camp experience. Chicken is pounded thin and fried to a crispy crust, making it perfect to enjoy with simple spaghetti and tomato sauce. This dish proves that you can make elegant meals over the fire without much effort.

SERVES 3

1½ pounds chicken breasts
Kosher salt
Black pepper
2 cups Italian bread crumbs
½ cup freshly grated Parmesan, divided
1 tablespoon dried basil
1 tablespoon dried oregano
2 eggs
Vegetable oil
One 24-ounce jar marinara sauce
8 ounces sliced fresh mozzarella
One 16-ounce box spaghetti, cooked
Chopped fresh parsley, for serving

1   On a large cutting board, trim your chicken breasts. Place a sheet of parchment paper on top and use a meat mallet to flatten them to about ½-inch thick. Season the chicken on both sides with salt and pepper.

2   In a small casserole dish, mix the bread crumbs, ¼ cup Parmesan, basil, and oregano. In a separate dish, whisk the eggs.

3   Dip each chicken breast into the egg and then into the bread crumb mixture.

4   Place a large skillet over medium heat, then pour in about ½ inch of vegetable oil. Heat the oil to 350°F.

5   Add the chicken and fry until golden brown, 4 to 5 minutes on each side.

6   Using a slotted spatula or spoon, transfer the chicken to a paper towel–lined plate.

7   Transfer the used vegetable oil to a glass container to discard. Wipe the skillet clean.

8   Pour half of the marinara sauce into the skillet. Add the fried chicken to the sauce and top the chicken with fresh mozzarella slices. Pour the remaining sauce over top.

9   Place the skillet over medium heat, cover, and cook until the mozzarella is melted, 10 minutes.

10   Serve the chicken over spaghetti and top with the remaining Parmesan and the parsley. Enjoy!

PARMESAN STEAK FRIES

The rustic and smoky flavor of a campfire pairs perfectly with these cheesy, garlicky, crispy campfire fries. The skillet gives them the crust that you just can't get in the oven.

SERVES 4 TO 6

4 large russet potatoes
4 tablespoons olive oil, divided
1 tablespoon unsalted butter, melted
⅓ cup grated Parmesan
1 tablespoon fresh thyme leaves
1 teaspoon kosher salt
½ teaspoon black pepper
4 garlic cloves, minced
2 tablespoons chopped fresh parsley

1 On a large cutting board, quarter each potato lengthwise. Place each quarter cut side up and slice down the middle lengthwise again.

2 In a large bowl, add 2 tablespoons of olive oil, the butter, Parmesan, thyme, salt, and pepper to the bowl.

3 Add the potato wedges to the bowl and toss to coat.

4 Add the remaining 2 tablespoons of olive oil to a large skillet and heat over the fire to about 350°F.

5 Carefully place the seasoned steak fries into the hot oil and cook until they start to get golden brown, about 10 minutes.

6 Add the garlic to the skillet. Cook the potatoes until evenly cooked and crispy, making sure to flip and move them around as needed, for about 10 more minutes.

7 Using a slotted spoon or spatula, transfer your fries to a paper towel–lined plate.

8 Top with chopped parsley and enjoy!

CAMPFIRE MEXICAN PIZZA

A recipe that satisfies those fast-food cravings while embracing the rustic charm of outdoor cooking. With a smoky crust, melted cheese, and fresh, zesty toppings, this pizza is like taco night, pressed between two tortillas and fried over a crackling campfire. Covering the pizza with a lid or some aluminum foil can help melt the cheese and cook the toppings more evenly.

SERVES 4

1 pound ground beef
1 tablespoon taco seasoning
½ cup vegetable oil
8 medium flour tortillas
One 16-ounce can refried beans
One 10-ounce can red enchilada sauce
1 cup shredded Mexican blend cheese
½ cup sour cream
1 medium tomato, diced
1 cup sliced black olives
2 green onions, sliced

1 In a large skillet over medium-high heat, brown the ground beef until no longer pink, 7 to 8 minutes. Drain the grease into a disposable container.

2 Stir in the taco seasoning and ½ cup water and simmer until the water is absorbed and the seasoning is fully incorporated, 5 minutes.

3 In another large skillet, heat the vegetable oil over medium heat. Add the tortillas and fry until they start to turn golden, about 1 minute per side. Transfer to a plate, then remove the skillet from the fire and discard the oil.

4 In a small skillet, warm the refried beans over medium heat, 3 to 4 minutes, stirring occasionally.

5 Spread a layer of refried beans on top of one tortilla, then one fourth of the ground beef. Place the other tortilla on top, then spoon a few tablespoons of enchilada sauce on top and sprinkle with ¼ cup of cheese. Repeat with the remaining tortillas, beans, beef, enchilada sauce, and cheese, to form four pizzas.

6 Place the large skillet back on the fire over medium heat.

7 Place an assembled pizza in the skillet and cover. Cook until the cheese is melted on top, 3 to 5 minutes. Remove from the heat. Repeat with the remaining pizzas.

8 Top with sour cream, tomato, olives, and green onions. Enjoy!

DUTCH OVEN

DUTCH OVEN NACHOS

A properly built nacho should be robust enough to handle the weight of its own toppings. These Dutch oven nachos can handle the weight of the world, and the flavor will transport you into an out-of-body experience. Grounded only by the colorful array of toppings, paired with melted cheese, salsa, and sour cream, this is a great dish to pass around the campfire or dinner table.

SERVES 4 TO 5

1 pound ground beef
One 1-ounce packet taco seasoning
One 12-ounce bag thick and sturdy
  tortilla chips
1 green bell pepper, diced
1 red bell pepper, diced
1 jalapeño, sliced
½ white onion, diced
2 cups shredded cheddar

For Serving
Sour cream
Salsa

1   In a medium skillet over medium-high heat, brown the beef, breaking it up with a wooden spoon, for 7 to 8 minutes. Drain the excess fat.

2   Stir in ⅔ cup water and the taco seasoning. Bring to a simmer for 3 minutes. Remove from the heat and set aside.

3   In a large Dutch oven, layer one-third of the tortilla chips, beef, bell peppers, jalapeño, onions, and cheddar.

4   Repeat the layering process twice more with the remaining ingredients.

5   Cover and cook over the fire on medium-high heat for 15 to 20 minutes, until the veggies have softened and the cheese is melted.

6   Remove from the heat. Top with salsa and sour cream and enjoy!

CAMPFIRE LASAGNA

The subtle flavor of a smoky campfire sets this recipe apart from any lasagna cooked in a conventional oven. A deer camp favorite, it's usually enjoyed around a fire, under a canopy of stars, with the chorus of night sounds and old buck stories. When you place this delicious meal at the center of your table, with your best buddies gathered around, I hope it's a catalyst for a good story or two. I know it's been for me!

SERVES 5 TO 6

1 egg
One 15-ounce container ricotta
¼ cup chopped fresh flat-leaf parsley
1 tablespoon Italian seasoning
½ teaspoon kosher salt
1 pound ground Italian pork sausage
1 tablespoon olive oil
One 25-ounce jar pasta sauce
One 9-ounce box oven-ready
  lasagna noodles
1½ cups shredded Italian blend
  cheese, divided

1 In a medium bowl, whisk the egg. Mix in the ricotta, parsley, Italian seasoning, and salt.

2 Place a Dutch oven over medium-high heat. Add the sausage to brown, breaking up the meat with a wooden spoon, 5 to 6 minutes. Transfer to a bowl and set aside.

3 To the Dutch oven, add the olive oil and ½ cup pasta sauce.

4 Arrange one layer of lasagna noodles over the sauce, breaking up the noodles into large pieces if needed, then top with another ½ cup sauce, half of the ricotta, ½ cup Italian cheese, and half of the sausage.

5 Repeat step 4 to add another layer.

6 For the top layer, add another layer of lasagna noodles, the remaining sauce, and the remaining cheese.

7 Cover the Dutch oven and place a few hot coals on top of the lid. Cook for about 30 minutes, rotating occasionally, until the lasagna is cooked through and the cheese is bubbly.

8 Remove from the heat and let rest for 5 minutes before you slice up and enjoy!

COLD POP PINEAPPLE UPSIDE-DOWN CAKE

You're going to want to gather everyone in the neighborhood, tailgate, or campground before flipping over your Dutch oven and revealing this lovely cake! I developed this recipe from an old Boy Scout recipe I used to make, but with water instead of cold pop. I've found that not only does the pop add a distinct flavor, it also helps keep the cake moist and fresh.

SERVES 6 TO 8

8 tablespoons (1 stick) unsalted butter
1 cup brown sugar
One 10-ounce can sliced pineapple
Maraschino cherries, stemmed
One 15.25-ounce box yellow cake mix
One 12-ounce can cold pop (I use ginger ale)

1 Melt the butter in a Dutch oven over medium heat. Stir in the brown sugar.

2 Place the pineapple rings over top of the brown sugar mixture, covering the entire bottom of the Dutch oven but not overlapping. Place a cherry inside each pineapple ring.

3 Pour the cake mix evenly over top of the pineapple. Gently pour the pop over top of the cake mix.

4 Cook for about 20 minutes, watching the cake as it bakes. Once the top of the cake rises, insert a knife into the center. If it comes out clean, the cake is done. Remove the Dutch oven from the fire and set aside for 5 minutes.

5 Using gloves, place a large cutting board on top of the Dutch oven. Flip and let the cake fall onto the board. Scrape any leftover fruit or topping off the bottom of the Dutch oven and add to the top of the cake. Enjoy!

CINNAMON PECAN ROLLS

The Dutch oven gives the outside of these cinnamon pecan rolls a buttery, crispy crust that complements both the sweetness of the cinnamon and the crunch of the pecans. Drizzled with tree juice, the thought of these rolls will roll you out of your sleeping bag or bed and into your apron. Surely you'll impress everybody enough to take the rest of the day off, buddy—enjoy it!

MAKES 12 ROLLS

All-purpose flour, for dusting
1 pound refrigerated pizza dough
6 tablespoons (¾ stick) softened
  butter, plus more for greasing
½ cup pecan halves
¾ cup brown sugar
2 tablespoons ground cinnamon
Pinch of kosher salt
Unflavored dental floss, for slicing
Grade A tree juice (maple syrup),
  for serving

1. Onto a large, lightly floured cutting board, roll out the pizza dough to a large rectangle, about 12 x 18 inches.

2. Spread the butter evenly onto the pizza dough.

3. Place the pecans in a zipper bag and use a mallet, someone's elbows, or a steel-toed boot to crush them into small pieces.

4. In a medium bowl, mix the brown sugar, pecans, cinnamon, and salt. Sprinkle evenly over top of the pizza dough.

5. Starting with the long end of the dough, roll the dough into a log. Pinch the ends and seal the seam with your fingers.

6. Use the dental floss or a sharp serrated knife to cut the log into 1½-inch slices to form your rolls.

7. Butter the bottom of a large Dutch oven and place the rolls in one layer on the bottom.

8. Cover and let the dough rise in a warm place for 30 minutes.

9. Place the Dutch oven over medium heat and bake for 30 to 35 minutes, checking on the rolls occasionally, until golden brown.

10. Remove from the heat, drizzle with tree juice, and enjoy!

COLD POP CHOCOLATE CARAMEL LAVA CAKE

Like my seventh-grade science fair volcano, this recipe is a ribbon winner (it also oozes caramel and chocolate lava). This cake is so simple and quick to make that you'll be whipping it up for your buddies around the campfire at midnight. It's even better when served with vanilla bean ice cream or a tall glass of cold milk.

SERVES 6 TO 8

One 12-ounce jar caramel topping
One 15.25-ounce box devil's food cake mix
One 12-ounce can cold pop (I use lemon-lime soda)
One 12-ounce bag semisweet chocolate chips
1 cup pecan halves

1 Pour the caramel sauce in an even layer across the bottom of a large Dutch oven.

2 Sprinkle the cake mix on top of the caramel. Slowly pour the cold pop over the cake mix.

3 Sprinkle in the chocolate chips, without stirring, then pecans on top.

4 Cover with a lid and cook over medium heat for 40 to 50 minutes, checking occasionally, until a knife inserted into the center of the cake comes out clean.

5 Remove from the heat and enjoy!

CHILI MAC

This chili mac recipe is a one-pot wonder that pairs the warm and hearty comfort of chili with the creamy, cheesy taste of mac and cheese. Green chiles, cumin, and chili powder create a gentle heat, balanced with succulent and tender slow-cooked ground beef. Serve with bread and butter, vegetables, or a fresh salad for a balanced meal.

SERVES 8 TO 10

1 tablespoon vegetable oil
1 pound ground beef
1 medium onion, finely diced
1¾ teaspoons chili powder
1½ teaspoons ground cumin
½ teaspoon kosher salt
3 garlic cloves, minced or grated
1 tablespoon brown sugar
One 15-ounce can tomato sauce
8 ounces elbow macaroni
1 cup frozen corn
One 4-ounce can diced green chiles
2 tablespoons chopped fresh cilantro
2 cups shredded Monterey Jack, divided

1   Heat a Dutch oven over medium-high heat and add the vegetable oil. Add the beef, onion, chili powder, cumin, and salt. Cook until the beef is browned, breaking up the meat with a wooden spoon, 7 to 8 minutes.

2   Add the garlic and brown sugar, and stir for 30 seconds. Stir in the tomato sauce, 2 cups water, and the macaroni. Cover and simmer for about 15 minutes, until the pasta is cooked through.

3   Stir in the corn, green chiles, cilantro, and 1 cup of cheese. Simmer until the cheese is melted, about 5 minutes.

4   Remove from the heat. Top with the remaining cheese and enjoy!

CHEESY SHREDDED POTATOES

The best part about cooking these cheesy potatoes over the fire is the crispy crust the Dutch oven gives them. Topped with more cheese and bread crumbs, this side dish will steal the show.

SERVES 8 TO 10

8 tablespoons (1 stick) salted butter

One 16-ounce container sour cream

One 10.5-ounce can cream of chicken soup

One 30-ounce bag frozen shredded hash browns, thawed

¼ onion, diced

4 cups shredded cheddar

1½ cups panko bread crumbs

1 In a small skillet over medium-high heat, melt the butter. Transfer ¼ cup of the butter to a medium bowl.

2 Add the sour cream and cream of chicken soup to the bowl and mix.

3 In a large Dutch oven, layer one-third of the hash browns, followed by one-third of the soup mixture, one-third of the onions, and one-third of the cheddar. Repeat the layering process until you've used all of the ingredients, ending with cheddar on top.

4 Make the topping: In a large bowl, mix the panko and the remaining ¼ cup melted butter until fully coated.

5 Evenly sprinkle the panko mixture over top and cover.

6 Cook over medium heat for about 20 minutes, until the topping is crispy and the mixture is bubbly and heated through. Enjoy!

QUESO DIP

This cheesy chip dip is hard to stop eating and won't last long around the bonfire. It's spicy and perfect with tortilla chips or even pretzel rods. Better make a couple batches, eh?

SERVES 8 TO 10

1 pound ground beef

One 1-ounce packet taco seasoning

One 16-ounce block Velveeta, diced into 1-inch cubes

One 15-ounce can black beans, drained

12 ounces pepper jack, diced into 1-inch cubes

2 cups salsa

One 4-ounce can jalapeño slices

Tortilla chips, for serving

1 Place a medium Dutch oven over medium-high heat. Add the beef and cook until browned, breaking up the meat with a wooden spoon, 7 to 8 minutes.

2 Drain the grease into a glass container for disposal.

3 Mix in ⅔ cup water and taco seasoning, reduce the heat to medium-low and simmer for 3 minutes.

4 Add the Velveeta, beans, pepper jack, salsa, and jalapeños. Let simmer for 5 to 10 minutes, stirring occasionally, until the cheese is melted and all of the ingredients are incorporated.

5 Serve warm with tortilla chips and enjoy!

COLD POP PUMPKIN PIE CAKE

A cold pop classic! This cake is full of earthy pumpkin flavor that will bring your campfire to the next level on a cool night. Grab a lantern, a blanket, and your coziest flannel and enjoy a slice sitting on top of a fresh-cut log around the fire.

SERVES 6 TO 8

Cooking spray
One 15-ounce can pumpkin puree
One 12-ounce can evaporated milk
2 eggs
1 teaspoon pumpkin pie spice
One 15.25-ounce box yellow cake mix
Half of a 12-ounce can cold pop (I use
   lemon-lime soda)
¾ cup chopped pecans

1 Spray a large Dutch oven with cooking spray.

2 In a large bowl, whisk together the pumpkin puree, evaporated milk, eggs, and pumpkin pie spice. Pour the mixture evenly into the bottom of the Dutch oven.

3 Layer the dry yellow cake mix over the pumpkin mixture. Without mixing, slowly pour cold pop over top of the cake mix. Top with the pecans.

4 Cover the Dutch oven and set over hot coals or embers. Place hot charcoals on top of the lid.

5 Cook for about 45 minutes, or until a knife inserted into the center comes out clean.

6 Remove from the heat and enjoy!

PUDGY PIES

EGG IN A HOLE PUDGY PIE

Sometimes it's the simplest things that taste the best, and this Boy Scout classic is no exception. You can't go wrong with eggs and toast, especially when you make the egg right inside the toast. Don't forget to use the leftover bread circle to soak up the extra butter and egg in the pan!

SERVES 1

Nonstick cooking spray
1 slice brioche bread
½ tablespoon butter
1 large egg
Kosher salt
Black pepper

1 Prep the pie iron by spraying the inside of both sides with cooking spray.

2 Cut a 2-inch circle out of the middle of the bread slice using a sharp knife or the top of a mason jar.

3 Butter both sides of the bread, then place the bread into the pie iron.

4 Crack the egg carefully into the hole in the center of the bread. Season with salt and black pepper.

5 Close and clamp the pie iron and, without turning it, carefully cook flat over hot coals for 2 to 5 minutes, until the bread is lightly toasted and the egg white is set.

6 Open up the pie iron to check on your egg and toast, then close and flip the pie iron and cook for an additional minute if needed, to make sure the bread is toasted and the egg is cooked.

7 Remove the pie iron from heat and transfer the pudgy pie to a plate. Enjoy!

CHEESY TOTS PUDGY PIE

This delicious breakfast treat is also one of my favorite late-night snacks! The toasted shell on the outside provides a crunchy contrast to the soft, cheesy filling inside. A twist on a school cafeteria staple, this recipe will take you back to when your biggest worry was a pop quiz.

SERVES 8

Nonstick cooking spray
One 32-ounce package frozen tater tots, thawed
Garlic salt
Black pepper
½ cup diced bell pepper
4 strips cooked bacon, crumbled
½ cup shredded Mexican blend cheese
Ranch dressing
¼ cup chopped chives

1 Prep the pie iron by spraying the inside of both sides with cooking spray.

2 Arrange 12 tater tots in rows along the bottom of one side of the pie iron. Sprinkle with garlic salt and black pepper.

3 Over top of the tots, add 1 tablespoon each of bell pepper, bacon, and cheese.

4 Close and clamp the pie iron and cook over hot coals for 4 to 5 minutes on each side, until the tots are toasted and the cheese has melted.

5 Remove from the heat and open up the pie iron. Transfer your pudgy pie to a plate.

6 Repeat steps 1 through 5 to make seven more pudgy pies.

7 Drizzle with ranch dressing and sprinkle with chives. Enjoy!

PUDGY PIE OMELET

A pudgy pie iron makes the perfect personal omelet. You can make these omelets however you want, making them a great option for a big group. They're delicious with spinach, tomatoes, mushrooms, and any kind of cheese you like, buddy!

SERVES 2

Nonstick cooking spray
3 eggs
Kosher salt
Black pepper
4 ounces diced ham
⅔ cup diced bell pepper
⅓ cup diced onion
½ cup shredded cheddar
Hot sauce, for serving

1 Prep the pie iron by spraying the inside of both sides with cooking spray.

2 In a medium bowl, whisk the eggs and season with salt and black pepper.

3 Pour the egg mixture into one side of the pie iron. Sprinkle in the ham, bell pepper, and onion and top with the cheddar.

4 Carefully place and clamp the top pie iron without flipping, or the eggs will run out of the iron.

5 Lay the pie iron flat over hot coals for 1 to 2 minutes. Carefully open the pie iron to check on the cooking progress, then cook until the egg is set, another 1 to 2 minutes.

6 Remove from the heat and transfer to a plate.

7 Repeat steps 3 through 6 to make another omelet. Top with hot sauce and enjoy!

TACO PUDGY PIE

Everything you love about tacos, sealed together in its own perfectly toasted pouch and made for easy eating! This is one of my all-time favorite recipes that I always recommend to people who are just getting into cooking pudgy pies. It will elevate your entire camping experience.

SERVES 8

½ pound ground beef

One 1-ounce packet taco seasoning mix

Nonstick cooking spray

Sixteen 5-inch street taco tortillas

½ cup finely chopped onion

1 cup shredded Mexican blend cheese

For Serving

Shredded lettuce

Diced tomatoes

Sliced black olives

Salsa

Sour cream

1 In a medium skillet over medium-high heat, brown the beef for 7 to 8 minutes, breaking up the meat with a wooden spoon. Drain the excess grease into a glass container for disposal.

2 Pour in ⅔ cup water and stir in the taco seasoning. Simmer for 3 to 4 minutes, until the water is absorbed and the seasoning is fully incorporated. Remove from the heat and set aside to cool.

3 Prep the pie iron by spraying the inside of both sides with cooking spray.

4 Place a tortilla on one side of the pie iron, then add about 2 tablespoons of the prepared beef. Sprinkle about 1 tablespoon of onion and 2 tablespoons of cheese over top.

5 Place the other tortilla over top. The tortilla should extend outside of the pie iron.

6 Close and clamp the pie iron. Cook over medium-hot coals for about 10 minutes, flipping halfway, until the tortilla is crispy.

7 Remove the pie iron from the heat and transfer the pudgy pie to a plate.

8 Top with lettuce, tomato, olives, salsa, and sour cream. Enjoy!

QUESADILLA BURGER PUDGY PIE

This burger is a lot to pack into the pie iron, so use your foot if you have to, buddy! Trust me, you'll be glad you made it work. The thin and crispy tortillas with melted pepper jack cheese makes this a different and refreshing take on a classic burger. Perfect for the big game, watching a classic film, or with a decent view.

SERVES 4

Mexi-Ranch Sauce
½ cup ranch dressing
½ cup sour cream
¼ cup salsa
1 teaspoon taco seasoning

Quesadilla Burgers
Sixteen 5-inch street taco tortillas
1½ cups shredded cheddar
1 pound ground beef
1 teaspoon kosher salt
½ teaspoon black pepper
Nonstick cooking spray
4 slices pepper jack
½ cup pico de gallo
1 cup shredded iceberg lettuce

1 **Prepare the Mexi-ranch sauce:** In a medium bowl, mix the ranch dressing, sour cream, salsa, and taco seasoning. Stir well and set aside for burger assembly.

2 **Make the quesadilla burgers:** Place four tortillas into a large skillet over medium heat and sprinkle about 3 tablespoons of cheddar over top of each. Top with four more tortillas and cook until the cheese has melted, about 2 minutes per side. Remove from the skillet, then repeat with the remaining tortillas and cheese. Set aside.

3 In a large bowl, combine the beef, salt, and pepper to taste. Divide into fourths and form into four patties, about 5 inches in diameter.

4 In the same skillet over medium heat, cook the patties until charred and cooked through, 4 to 5 minutes per side. Remove from the heat and transfer to a plate.

5 Prep a large pie iron by spraying the inside of both sides with cooking spray.

6 Place one quesadilla on one side of the pie iron.

7 Place a cooked burger on top. Layer with a pepper jack cheese slice and 2 tablespoons each of pico de gallo, shredded lettuce, and Mexi-ranch sauce. Top with the other cheese quesadilla.

8 Close and clamp the pie iron. Cook over medium hot coals for about 5 minutes, until the tortillas are crispy, flipping halfway through.

9 Open the pie iron, remove the burger from the heat, and transfer to a plate.

10 Repeat steps 5 through 9 to form three more quesadilla burgers. Enjoy with extra Mexi-ranch sauce.

MEATLOAF PUDGY PIE

A blue collar, hearty, homestyle supper all packed inside your own personal pie iron. For me, it's like bringing a piece of home to my campfire, with every bite transporting me back to simpler times, spent at my mother's kitchen table.

SERVES 4

Meatloaf Seasoning

2 teaspoons ground mustard
2 teaspoons paprika
1 teaspoon dried basil
1 teaspoon garlic powder
1 teaspoon onion powder
1 teaspoon black pepper
½ teaspoon kosher salt
¼ teaspoon dried thyme

Meatloaf

1 pound ground beef
1 pound ground pork
3 large eggs
⅓ cup ketchup
2 teaspoons Worcestershire sauce
1 cup soft bread crumbs
Nonstick cooking spray
BBQ sauce

1 **Make the seasoning:** In a large bowl, mix the mustard, paprika, basil, garlic powder, onion powder, black pepper, salt, and thyme until well combined.

2 **Make the meatloaf:** To the bowl, add the beef, pork, eggs, ketchup, Worcestershire sauce, and bread crumbs, using your hands to incorporate well. Form the mixture into four tightly packed loaves.

3 Prepare the pie iron by covering both sides with aluminum foil and spraying with cooking spray.

4 Place one of the loaves into the pie iron.

5 Glaze one side of the meatloaf with BBQ sauce and close the pie iron.

6 Cook over hot coals for 30 to 35 minutes, flipping halfway through. Check on the meatloaf after about 25 minutes and adjust the cooking time accordingly.

7 Remove the pie iron from the heat, then open it and transfer the meatloaf to a plate.

8 Repeat steps 3 through 7 to make three more meatloaves. Enjoy!

CARAMEL APPLE PUDGY PIE

With the flavors of autumn pressed into a pie iron, this pudgy pie will put you in your feels. Maybe it's the aroma of caramelizing sugar and baking apples filling the air. Maybe it's the taste of tart apples and gooey caramel or the nostalgia of cooking over an open fire. Whatever it is, it won't matter when you're eating this delicious treat!

SERVES 1

Nonstick cooking spray
Salted butter, softened
2 slices white bread
¼ cup apple pie filling
½ teaspoon ground cinnamon
2 tablespoons caramel sundae syrup

1   Prep the pie iron by spraying the inside of both sides with cooking spray.

2   Spread butter on one side of one slice of bread. Place it butter side down in the pie iron.

3   Spread the apple pie filling on top of the bread, then sprinkle with cinnamon. Top with caramel syrup.

4   Spread butter on one side of the other piece of bread and place it butter side up on top of the apple, cinnamon, and caramel mixture.

5   Close and clamp the pie iron and cook over hot coals for 1 to 2 minutes on each side, until toasted and heated through. Open the pie iron to check on it; if it needs more time, close and cook for another few minutes. You can open up the pie iron to check on it about halfway through.

6   Remove from the heat and open up the pie iron. Transfer your pudgy pie to a plate and enjoy!

STUFFED CORNBREAD PUDGY PIE

Smoke your own pulled pork or use some leftovers to stuff inside this sweet cornbread pie recipe. It combines buttery golden cornbread and the taste of smoky barbecue. Add some spice with pepper jack cheese and enjoy fireside with a couple cold pops.

SERVES 4

2 eggs
Two 8.5-ounce boxes corn muffin mix
1 cup milk
¼ cup melted butter or oil
One 4-ounce can diced green chiles
Nonstick cooking spray
2 cups pulled pork
4 slices pepper jack

1   In a large bowl, whisk the eggs. Add the muffin mix, milk, and butter and stir to combine. Stir in the green chiles.

2   Prepare the pie iron by spraying the inside of both sides with cooking spray.

3   Pour ¼ cup of the cornbread mixture into the bottom of the pie iron. Add the pulled pork and pepper jack on top. Top it off with another ¼ cup of cornbread mixture.

4   Close and clamp the pie iron, keeping the pie iron face up and level. Place the iron over hot coals and cook for 15 minutes, until the cornbread is cooked through and golden brown, flipping halfway through.

5   Open the pie iron, remove the pie, and transfer to a plate. Enjoy!

FAJITA PUDGY PIE

Packed with sautéed peppers and onions and topped with melty cheese, this is a great handheld alternative to your average fajita and a lot more fun to make.

SERVES 4

1 tablespoon olive oil
Rainbow of small bell peppers (red, green, and yellow), thinly sliced
Eight 5-inch flour tortillas
1 medium onion, thinly sliced
One 1-ounce packet fajita seasoning mix
Nonstick cooking spray
1 cup shredded Mexican blend cheese

For Serving
Salsa
Guacamole

1 Place a medium skillet over medium-high heat. Heat the olive oil, then add the peppers and onions. Sauté until the onions are translucent and the peppers are tender-crisp, about 7 minutes.

2 Mix in the fajita seasoning and cook until the veggies are tender and slightly charred and the seasoning is fully incorporated, another 2 minutes. Remove from the heat and set aside.

3 Prepare the pie iron by spraying the inside of both sides with cooking spray.

4 Place a tortilla in one side of the pie iron and fill with about ¼ cup each of the shredded cheese and the veggie fajita mixture. Top with another tortilla, then close and clamp the pie iron.

5 Heat over the fire, turning occasionally, until the tortilla is toasted and the cheese is melted, about 10 minutes.

6 Remove from the heat and transfer the pie to a plate. Serve with salsa and guacamole and enjoy!

MUTTER BUTTER PUDGY PIE

This nostalgic treat definitely satisfies your sweet tooth, with milk chocolate, peanut butter, banana, and marshmallows. I originally made this recipe in Boy Scouts. It will always hold a special place in my heart and in my campfire dessert lineup.

SERVES 1

Nonstick cooking spray
2 slices white bread
¼ cup peanut butter
1 ounce milk chocolate
¼ cup mini marshmallows
1 banana, sliced

1 Prepare the pie iron by spraying the inside of both sides with cooking spray.

2 Spread one side of one piece of bread with peanut butter. Place the bread into the pie iron, peanut butter side up.

3 Break apart the chocolate and place the pieces over top of the peanut butter. Add a layer of mini marshmallows and sliced bananas.

4 Top with the other piece of bread. Close and clamp the pie iron.

5 Cook over hot coals for about 3 minutes, then flip and cook the other side for 3 more minutes, until the bread is toasted.

6 Remove from the heat, transfer the pie to a plate, and enjoy!

FOIL PACKS

CHEESESTEAK FOIL PACK

I like to prepare these personal supper packs before a hike, placing them in a container inside my bag. When hunger strikes, I can easily pull them out and roast over a hot campfire, creek-side preferably. With steak, provolone, onions, and peppers, this foil pack smells like the parking lot before a Flyers-Penguins game. Grab a fork and knife and enjoy right out of the foil or on a warm hoagie roll.

SERVES 4

1 red bell pepper, thinly sliced
1 green bell pepper, thinly sliced
1 medium yellow onion, thinly sliced
1 pound steak, thinly sliced
3 tablespoons olive oil
2 teaspoons Italian seasoning
Kosher salt
Black pepper
Nonstick cooking spray
4 slices provolone
4 hoagie rolls

1 To a large bowl, add the bell peppers and onion, then add the steak.

2 Add the olive oil, Italian seasoning, and salt and black pepper to taste. Mix well to coat.

3 Cut heavy-duty aluminum foil into two large rectangles. Spray one side of each rectangle with cooking spray, then add the steak, pepper and onion mixture to one of the rectangles. Place the other foil rectangle on top, sprayed side down, then seal the edges to form a pack.

4 Set the foil pack over hot coals and cook for 12 to 15 minutes, until the peppers are softened and the steak is cooked through. Remove and open the foil pack to check to see if it's cooked; if not, place the pack over the hot coals for a few more minutes.

5 Remove from the heat, open the foil pack, and cover with the provolone slices. Close the foil pack back up and allow for the cheese to melt, 3 to 4 minutes.

6 Transfer the cheesesteak to the hoagie rolls or enjoy straight from the foil pack.

MONKEY BREAD FOIL PACK

A variation on my skillet Monkey Bread (on page 123), this version wraps all of the flavors into a tight foil pack. These cinnamon sugar–packed bites are fun to make and are perfect for sharing with a large group around the campfire.

SERVES 6

One 12.4-ounce can refrigerated cinnamon rolls with icing
¼ cup granulated sugar
1 teaspoon ground cinnamon
Nonstick cooking spray
4 tablespoons (½ stick) cold butter, diced
½ cup brown sugar

1 Cut each cinnamon roll into fourths.

2 To a large zipper bag, add the granulated sugar and cinnamon. Shake to combine.

3 Add the cinnamon rolls to the bag. Seal and shake to coat each piece with the cinnamon sugar.

4 Cut heavy-duty aluminum foil into four medium square pieces. Spray one side of each square with cooking spray.

5 Divide the cinnamon roll pieces in half and place onto the sprayed side of two of the foil squares.

6 Divide and sprinkle the butter equally on top of the cinnamon roll pieces. Sprinkle ¼ cup of brown sugar on top of each foil pack.

7 Cover each foil pack with the other piece of foil (with the sprayed side down), then fold the edges up to form sealed packs.

8 Place the packs over hot coals for 15 to 20 minutes until the bread is golden and puffy.

9 Remove the packs from the heat, then open them up and drizzle with icing. Enjoy!

FOIL TORTILLA DESSERT WRAPS

These wraps are an easy and sweet finish to the night. Coconut, marshmallow, and milk chocolate all melt together while wrapped in a warm and toasty tortilla.

SERVES 3

Three 8-inch flour tortillas
1 cup mini marshmallows
1 cup milk chocolate chips
1 cup unsweetened coconut flakes
Whipped cream, for serving

1   Lay a tortilla flat on a large square of heavy-duty aluminum foil. On half of the tortilla, sprinkle about $1/3$ cup each of marshmallows, chocolate chips, and coconut flakes.

2   Tuck in the sides, then roll up the tortilla into a burrito. Tightly wrap the tortilla in the aluminum foil.

3   Repeat steps 1 and 2 with the remaining tortillas, marshmallows, chocolate chips, and coconut flakes.

4   Place the foil packs over hot coals and cook for 5 to 10 minutes, until the marshmallow and chocolate are melted and the tortilla is toasted and golden brown. Make sure to continually rotate the packs to prevent the tortillas from burning.

5   Remove from the heat. Unwrap the foil and top with whipped cream. Enjoy!

BBQ CHICKEN NACHOS FOIL PACK

Enjoy these nachos on your own or shared around the campfire. I like to use leftover BBQ chicken, making them quick to fold up into packs for a day hike. The fire really crisps the tortilla chips while melting the cheese onto the chicken.

SERVES 8 TO 10

Nonstick cooking spray
One 11-ounce bag tortilla chips
4 cups shredded Mexican blend cheese
3 cups pulled BBQ chicken
One 15-ounce can black beans, rinsed and drained
1 cup cooked sweet corn kernels
BBQ sauce

For Serving
Diced tomatoes
Guacamole
Sliced jalapeños
Sour cream
Salsa
Chopped cilantro

1   Cut heavy-duty aluminum foil into two large rectangles. Spray one side of each rectangle with cooking spray.

2   Fill one rectangle with one fourth of the tortilla chips. Sprinkle with one fourth of the cheese, then one fourth of the chicken. Top with a layer of black beans and corn. Drizzle with BBQ sauce to taste.

3   Repeat step 2 to add three more layers.

4   Place the other piece of foil over top and seal the edges to create a pack.

5   Place the pack over hot coals and cook for 5 to 6 minutes. Rotate the pack 180 degrees and cook for 2 minutes or until the cheese has melted.

6   Remove from the fire and open up the foil pack.

7   Top with diced tomatoes, guacamole, jalapeños, sour cream, salsa, and cilantro. Enjoy!

CHILI CHEESE FRIES FOIL PACK

I'm sure you've had chili cheese fries, but have you had them over the fire? Packed into your own personal foil pack for the ultimate late-night snack? If you're not sold yet, that's the best I can do, buddy, but if you do make them, make sure to have plenty of napkins nearby. Especially if you have a mustache.

SERVES 10 TO 12

Nonstick cooking spray
One 32-ounce package frozen
  regular-cut French fries
Sea salt
One 15-ounce can chili with beans
One 14.5-ounce can diced tomatoes,
  drained
1 cup freshly grated cheddar
Chopped chives, for serving

1   Cut heavy-duty aluminum foil into two large rectangles. Spray one side of each rectangle with cooking spray.

2   Place the French fries on top of one foil rectangle. Sprinkle with sea salt.

3   To a medium bowl, add the chili and tomatoes. Stir to combine.

4   Pour the chili mixture over the fries and sprinkle with cheese.

5   Place the other piece of foil over top and seal the edges to create a pack.

6   Place the pack on top of hot coals and cook for about 25 minutes or until the fries are fully cooked and the cheese is melted.

7   Transfer to a plate and top with chives. Enjoy!

FOILED SWEET POTATOES
WITH MARSHMALLOWS

These foil-packed treats give off a sweet aroma that will make your mouth water as they roast over the coals. Sprinkle them with cinnamon and/or brown sugar, and you've got a delicious snack for any time of day.

SERVES 4

4 large sweet potatoes
8 tablespoons (1 stick) butter
Ground cinnamon
Kosher salt
12 large marshmallows

1 Poke holes all over the sweet potatoes with a fork.

2 Wrap each potato in heavy-duty aluminum foil.

3 Place the potato packs over hot coals and cook for about 30 minutes, until the potatoes are cooked through.

4 Remove the packs from the coals and set aside to cool for 5 to 10 minutes. Unwrap the foil and cut the sweet potatoes lengthwise, being careful not to cut all the way through.

5 Add 2 tablespoons of butter to each potato and gently mash the inside with a fork until the butter has melted. Sprinkle each potato with cinnamon and salt to taste.

6 Roast the marshmallows over the fire and add three on top of each potato. Sprinkle the top with more cinnamon and enjoy!

COPPER MINER'S PASTY

These pasties, once a typical lunch for the copper miners of Michigan's Upper Peninsula, are a labor of love and well worth the work. Enjoy as the copper miners did by wrapping in foil, placing on a shovel, and heating over the fire until steaming inside.

SERVES 12

Dough
2 cups shortening
2 cups boiling water
5½ cups all-purpose flour, plus more for dusting
2 teaspoons kosher salt

Filling
1 pound ground beef
½ pound ground pork
6 medium red potatoes, peeled and diced
2 small rutabagas, peeled and diced
2 medium onions, diced
3 teaspoons kosher salt
2 teaspoons black pepper
2 teaspoons garlic powder
4 tablespoons (½ stick) butter
1 large egg, lightly beaten

1 **Make the dough:** In a large bowl, mix the shortening and boiling water until the shortening is melted. Slowly stir in the flour and salt to form a dough; cover with plastic wrap and place in the fridge for 1½ hours.

2 Preheat the oven to 350°F. Line a large baking sheet with parchment paper.

3 **Make the filling:** In a large bowl, gently combine and crumble the beef and pork. Add the potatoes, rutabagas, onions, salt, pepper, and garlic powder.

4 Take the dough out of the fridge and divide into 12 equal portions.

5 On a lightly floured surface, roll out one portion of dough into an 8-inch circle. Repeat with the remaining dough portions.

6 Spoon about 1 cup of filling onto half of each circle and top each with 1 teaspoon butter.

7 Moisten the edges of each circle with water and carefully fold the dough over the filling. Press the edges with a fork to seal.

8 Place the pasties onto the baking sheet. Cut three slits into the top of each pasty and brush with beaten egg. Bake for 1 hour or until golden brown.

9 Transfer the pasties to a wire rack to cool. Wrap each pasty in heavy-duty aluminum foil and refrigerate for up to 5 days.

10 To reheat over the campfire fire like the copper miners did, set the head of a metal shovel over top of the fire to heat. Place a foil-wrapped pasty on top of the shovel head.

11 Heat until the pasty is steaming and reaches an internal temperature of 165°F, 20 to 25 minutes.

12 Enjoy the old-fashioned way!

FRENCH DIP FOIL PACK

This sandwich has melted butter, garlic, provolone cheese, and roast beef, all roasting together over hot coals while tightly packed in foil. You can enjoy the whole sandwich yourself or slice it up to serve a group. Whatever you do, don't forget to dip it into the savory au jus gravy.

SERVES 2

One 12-inch French loaf
½ pound sliced deli roast beef
6 slices provolone
2 tablespoons butter
¼ teaspoon garlic powder
One 1-ounce packet au jus gravy mix

1 Slice the loaf lengthwise. Place the roast beef along the bottom of the bread. Top with the provolone.

2 In a small skillet, melt the butter over hot coals. Transfer the melted butter to a small bowl, add the garlic powder, and stir to combine.

3 Spread the garlic butter all over the inside of the top half of the bread. Close the sandwich.

4 Using heavy-duty aluminum foil, wrap the sandwich tightly. Make sure to close both ends of the foil pack.

5 Place the foil pack over indirect heat and cook for 20 to 25 minutes, until the cheese is melted and the bread is toasted.

6 Remove the foil pack from the coals and let cool.

7 Heat the au jus sauce packet with 3 cups of water in a medium skillet over the fire, just until it reaches a simmer.

8 Remove from the heat and serve with your sandwich. Enjoy!

FOIL JERK CHICKEN WINGS

Chicken wings are drenched in Caribbean jerk seasoning and sealed into a foil pack to steam and marinate over hot coals. Finish these off with a squeeze of lime, and don't forget the wet wipes.

SERVES 3 TO 4

Jerk Seasoning

1 tablespoon ground allspice
1 tablespoon cayenne
1 tablespoon ground cinnamon
1 tablespoon ground cumin
1 tablespoon garlic powder
1 tablespoon ground nutmeg
1 tablespoon savory seasoning
1 tablespoon smoked paprika
1 tablespoon dried parsley
1 tablespoon white pepper
2 teaspoons kosher salt
1 teaspoon brown sugar
1 teaspoon ground cloves

Chicken Wings

8 chicken wings, split
2 tablespoons vegetable oil
Nonstick cooking spray
1 lime, for serving

1 **Make the jerk seasoning:** In a medium bowl, combine the allspice, cayenne, cinnamon, cumin, garlic powder, nutmeg, savory seasoning, paprika, parsley, pepper, salt, brown sugar, and cloves. Mix well.

2 To a large bowl, add the chicken wings, vegetable oil, and about ¼ cup jerk seasoning (see Note) and toss to coatl.

3 Cut heavy-duty aluminum foil into two 18 x 24-inch rectangles. Spray one side of each rectangle with cooking spray.

4 Place the chicken wings onto one piece foil and cover with the other piece of foil. Seal the edges to make a pack.

5 Place the pack over hot coals and cook for about 25 minutes, rotating the pack often, until the chicken is cooked through.

6 Remove from the heat, transfer to a plate, and top with fresh squeezed lime juice. Enjoy!

Note: Save the rest of the jerk seasoning in an airtight container for later use. Store in a cool, dark place for up to 6 months.

FOILED MEXICAN STREET CORN

You won't want corn any other way after this. A little bit spicy, smoky, and cheesy, this corn—inspired by elote, the classic Mexican street food—will become a quick favorite around the fire or on the grill.

SERVES 8

8 ears corn, husked
8 tablespoons (1 stick) butter
Kosher salt
½ cup mayonnaise
½ cup sour cream
½ cup chopped cilantro, plus more for serving
1 garlic clove, minced
¼ teaspoon cayenne
¼ teaspoon ground cumin
¼ teaspoon garlic powder
Juice of 1 lime
½ cup crumbled cotija
½ teaspoon chili powder

1 Butter each ear of corn and sprinkle with salt.

2 Wrap each ear of corn in heavy-duty aluminum foil. Place over hot coals and grill for about 40 minutes, until tender.

3 In a small bowl, mix the mayonnaise, sour cream, cilantro, garlic, cayenne, cumin, garlic powder, and lime juice.

4 Remove the corn from the heat and open up the foil packs. Using a brush, coat each ear of corn with about 2 tablespoons of the mayo mixture and about 1 tablespoon of the cotija.

5 Sprinkle with cilantro and chili powder. Enjoy!

COMPANIONS

"Companions" is a term I use to refer to foods that complement the main course of a meal, things like appetizers, desserts, and drinks. I like to think of appetizers as the meal's first impression—a welcoming hello—and the dessert as the meal's closing remarks—a heartfelt goodbye. Drinks accompany the entire meal, transitioning us between courses and cleansing our palates.

The recipes in this section are not only meant to be shared with those closest to us, but can also be enjoyed alone, perhaps in the company of a good book, video game, TV show, or movie. Here in the Cedar Swamp, my Honey Cinnamon Cold Brew (on page 251) is best served while listening to Neil Young's *Harvest* album, while my grandmother's Reese's Bars (on page 226) pair perfectly with a classic film like *The Goonies*, *Hook*, or, for a longer commitment, the entire *Lord of the Rings* series. My Spinach Dip (on page 211) pairs well with *FIFA 96* on Sega Genesis or *Tony Hawk's Pro Skater 1* or *3* on PlayStation, and my Peach Lemonade (on page 248) is the perfect refreshment for flipping through a *Cosmopolitan* or *Field & Stream* magazine. My Aunt Martha's Brown Sugar & Nut Cake recipe (on page 222) is perfect with a good conversation or a decent view. No matter the occasion, outing, or event, these recipes are sure to help the vibe.

A cool thing about Companions is that they can be enjoyed by themselves as a delicious snack or together, in any order, as part of a hearty meal. My old Uncle Butch always has his dessert before dinner, and it's tough to dispute his reasoning that no doctor could prove that eating lemon meringue before a pot roast is worse than eating it after one. In fact,

making sure he had the room to enjoy that lemon meringue, which he deemed "one of the finer things in life," was a veteran move, really. I adopted the same practice as old Uncle Butch sometime in late high school, and I've done it ever since. This is the first time that I've admitted it to him, but if you're reading this Uncle Butch, well done and I love you.

Another cool thing about Companions is not only do they help balance out our meals, but they can also help bring balance to our life. For me, nothing is better than suddenly canceling all engagements, and all plans, to instead stay home and center my day around a movie marathon, eating a flawlessly executed batch of Grandpa Bob's Fudge (on page 229), paired with a cold glass of two-percent milk and a couple healthy naps on the sofa. Or perhaps spending the entire weekend getting caught up on a TV series while whipping up some carrot cakes and packing them into sturdy boxes to ship out via ground mail. Companions are a pleasure to prepare, a pleasure to serve, and obviously a pleasure to eat.

The following pages contain recipes that will likely sway first impressions, sales pitches, business negotiations, and job interviews in your favor. To quote Spider-Man's Uncle Ben, "With great power, comes great responsibility," so please use these recipes responsibly, buddy! In all seriousness, whether these Companions are served beside other recipes in this book, by themselves, or alongside one of your own family recipes, I hope they can help play a small role in bringing some amazing meals, moments, and memories to you and those closest to you.

APPETIZERS

FIVE MILLION DOLLAR DIP

Living up to its name, this dip delivers five million dollars worth of serious flavor. To most, it's a million-dollar dip, but my grandmother upped the ante. Incredibly easy to make, it's a great last-minute dip to mix up for friends.

SERVES 6 TO 8

8 ounces shredded cheddar
5 green onions, chopped
1½ cups mayonnaise
½ cup slivered almonds, toasted
½ cup real bacon bits
Crackers, for serving

1   To a medium bowl, add the cheddar, green onions, mayonnaise, almonds, and bacon bits. Mix well to combine.

2   Refrigerate for at least two hours. Serve with crackers and enjoy!

TACO DIP

All the taco fixin's in one hearty dip. You'll want to make sure you hit every layer with your tortilla chip, so pick a sturdy one. Think of it like a basement that will need to support seven floors of flavor.

SERVES 8

One 16-ounce can refried beans

One 16-ounce container guacamole (about 2 cups)

One 16-ounce container sour cream

8 ounces softened cream cheese

One 1-ounce packet taco seasoning

2 Roma tomatoes, chopped

1 cup shredded cheddar

One 2.25-ounce can sliced black olives, drained

2 green onions, chopped

Tortilla chips, for serving

1 To a 9-inch pie pan or 9-inch square baking dish, add the refried beans in an even layer, then add the guacamole in an even layer on top.

2 To a medium bowl, add the sour cream, cream cheese, and taco seasoning. Use a hand mixer to blend until smooth. Layer the mixture over top of the guacamole.

3 Layer on the tomatoes, cheese, and black olives. Top with green onions.

4 Enjoy right away or chill for an hour before serving with tortilla chips.

DEVILED EGGS

Sometimes it's best not to mess with a classic: these classic deviled eggs, sprinkled with paprika and cooked to perfection. These egg bites won't last very long, so maybe make a couple batches.

SERVES 6 TO 8

12 large eggs
½ cup avocado oil mayonnaise
2 teaspoons Dijon mustard
½ teaspoon smoked paprika, plus more for serving
½ teaspoon kosher salt

1 To hard-boil the eggs, bring a large pot of water to a gentle boil. Gently place the eggs directly from the cold fridge into the boiling water. Cook, uncovered, for 12 minutes.

2 Meanwhile, make an ice bath with ice and water in a large bowl.

3 Using tongs, transfer the eggs from the boiling water to the ice bath. Let the eggs cool enough to touch.

4 Gently roll each egg on the counter to crack the shell. Peel each egg, then halve lengthwise with a sharp paring knife and separate the yolks into a large bowl. Place the egg whites on a serving platter.

5 To the bowl with the yolks, add the mayonnaise, mustard, paprika, and salt. Using a fork, mash the yolks into the other ingredients until smooth.

6 Use a spoon to fill each egg white with a generous tablespoon of the mashed yolk mixture (you can also fill a zipper bag with the mixture, cut off the bottom corner, and pipe the mixture into the egg whites). Top with a sprinkle of paprika.

7 Serve right away or chill in the fridge before serving. Enjoy!

MAPLE BACON CRACKERS

A unique and addicting treat, these crackers are both savory and sweet. A match made in flavor heaven: maple bacon and brown sugar. Keep these crackers off your front seat when transporting; they're hard to stop eating.

SERVES 10 TO 12

50 rectangular butter crackers
1 pound maple bacon, chopped
1¼ cups light brown sugar
1¼ cup (2½ sticks) unsalted butter

1   Preheat the oven to 400°F. Line a large baking sheet with parchment paper, then cover with a single layer of crackers.

2   Add the bacon to a medium pan and cook over medium heat until crispy, 8 minutes. Transfer to a paper towel–lined plate and set aside.

3   To a saucepan, add the sugar and butter and bring to a boil until the sugar is dissolved and the butter is melted, 3 minutes, stirring occasionally.

4   Carefully pour the butter-sugar mixture over the crackers.

5   Place the baking sheet in the oven and bake for 5 minutes, until the butter-sugar mixture is bubbly.

6   Remove the baking sheet from the oven and sprinkle the bacon over top of the crackers. Set aside to cool, then break into pieces. Enjoy!

CHILI CHEESE DIP

The game's on and you need a quick snack. I got you, buddy. This hot chili cheese dip is a fun spin on chili cheese fries, served best with corn chips, potato chips, or even french fries.

SERVES 6 TO 8

8 ounces cream cheese, softened
One 15-ounce can chili without beans
One 4-ounce can diced green chiles
1 cup shredded Mexican blend cheese

For Serving
Sour cream
Chopped green onions
Corn chips or tortilla chips

1 To a microwave-safe pie plate, add the cream cheese in an even layer, then add the chili in an even layer on top. Add a layer of chiles and top with cheese.

2 Microwave for 3 to 4 minutes, until the cheese has melted.

3 Top with a dollop of sour cream, sprinkle with green onions, and serve with corn chips or tortilla chips. Enjoy!

BLT DIP

This cold dip tastes like you're eating a sandwich in every bite. Great with chips, crackers, or sliced baguette.

SERVES 4 TO 6

6 slices bacon, chopped
8 ounces cream cheese, softened
1 cup sour cream
One 1-ounce packet ranch seasoning
½ teaspoon garlic powder
½ cup shredded iceberg lettuce
1 Roma tomato, diced
1 cup shredded cheddar
Tortilla chips, for serving

1 In a medium pan over medium-low heat, cook the bacon until crispy, 8 to 10 minutes. Transfer to a paper towel–lined plate and set aside.

2 In a large mixing bowl, mix the cream cheese, sour cream, ranch seasoning, garlic powder, and most of the crispy bacon pieces. Save about ¼ cup of the bacon bits for topping.

3 Transfer the mixture to a pie plate and smooth it into an even layer.

4 Top with lettuce, tomatoes, and cheese. Sprinkle with the rest of your bacon pieces and enjoy with chips for dipping!

JALAPEÑO POPPER PIGS
(IN A BLANKET)

A spicy version of classic pigs in a blanket, these are an easy way to please a crowd. Jalapeño brine is used to add that extra kick to your pigs. Keep a cold pop nearby for extinguishment.

SERVES 6 TO 8

4 ounces cream cheese, softened

1 tablespoon jalapeño brine, from a can of pickled, sliced jalapeños

All-purpose flour, for dusting

One 8-ounce package crescent dough

½ cup shredded sharp cheddar

¼ cup canned pickled sliced jalapeños, finely chopped

10 beef hot dogs, cut into thirds

1 large egg

Kosher salt

1 Preheat the oven to 375°F. Line a baking sheet with parchment paper.

2 To a small bowl, add the cream cheese and jalapeño brine. Mix well until combined.

3 Sprinkle a clean surface with flour, unroll the crescent dough, and gently press it down flat. Spread the cream cheese over top, covering it completely. Top with cheddar. Sprinkle the jalapeños over top of the cheese.

4 With a sharp knife, cut the dough lengthwise into 1-inch strips, then cut the strips into fourths.

5 Add a piece of hot dog to each cut strip. Roll the hot dog up in the dough and seal the ends.

6 Place each roll onto the baking sheet, seam side down, leaving some space between rolls.

7 In a small bowl, whisk the egg with a splash of water. Using a brush, coat each roll on all sides. Top with a sprinkle of salt.

8 Bake for 15 minutes or until golden brown. Enjoy!

SPINACH DIP

Here you go, buddy. This dip is always a favorite at the potluck. If you make it, bring recipe cards—people will be asking for them. Slice up some toasted baguette and dip into the cheesy spinach goodness.

SERVES 6

Nonstick cooking spray
8 ounces cream cheese, softened
¾ cup sour cream
10 ounces frozen spinach, thawed and drained
1½ cups shredded mozzarella, divided
½ cup freshly grated Parmesan
1 tablespoon dried minced onion
2 teaspoons minced garlic
½ teaspoon kosher salt
¼ teaspoon black pepper
Sliced baguette, for serving

1 Preheat the oven to 400°F. Grease a medium baking dish with cooking spray.

2 To a large bowl, add the cream cheese and sour cream. Using an electric mixer, beat until smooth.

3 Stir in the spinach, ¾ cup mozzarella, the Parmesan, onion, garlic, salt, and pepper.

4 Transfer the mixture to the baking dish. Top with the remaining mozzarella.

5 Bake for about 20 minutes, until the cheese is melted and the dip is bubbly, then broil for 2 minutes to brown the cheese.

6 While the dip is cooling, toast the baguette slices on a baking sheet for about 5 minutes. Enjoy the dip with the baguette!

DESSERTS

SEVEN LAYER BARS

Wrap these bars in wax paper and ship them off to your best buddies or keep the recipe to yourself and savor those seven layers in secrecy. When you're craving something sweet and salty, there's no wrong time or place to eat a seven layer bar.

SERVES 9

½ cup melted butter
1 cup graham cracker crumbs
1 cup butterscotch chips
1 cup chocolate chips
1 cup chopped pecans
1 cup sweetened condensed milk
1 cup unsweetened shredded coconut

1 Preheat the oven to 350°F. Line an 8-inch square baking pan with parchment paper.

2 In a medium bowl, combine the melted butter and graham cracker crumbs. Press the mixture into the bottom of the pan.

3 Sprinkle on the butterscotch chips, chocolate chips, and pecans. Pour the condensed milk evenly over top, then sprinkle the coconut on top.

4 Bake for 30 minutes, until the coconut is toasted and the butterscotch and chocolate chips are fully melted, then set aside to cool before cutting into bars. Enjoy!

APPLE CAKE

A rock band of fall flavors. Every ingredient plays an important role in this recipe, but it's the apple that steals the show on vocals and lead guitar. Worthy of its fan base, this apple cake's a real crowd pleaser. Leave your audience satisfied with no encore needed.

SERVES 12

Nonstick cooking spray
2 cups all-purpose flour
1¾ cups sugar
1 teaspoon baking soda
1 teaspoon ground cinnamon
½ teaspoon kosher salt
1 cup melted vegetable shortening, such as Crisco
3 eggs
1 teaspoon vanilla extract
4 cups peeled and thinly sliced Granny Smith apples
¾ cup chopped nuts, such as pecans or walnuts

For Serving (optional)
Vanilla ice cream
Whipped cream

1 Preheat the oven to 350°F. Spray a 9 x 13-inch baking dish with cooking spray.

2 In a medium bowl, whisk together the flour, sugar, baking soda, cinnamon, and salt.

3 In a large bowl, mix together the shortening, eggs, and vanilla. Add the dry ingredients and stir to combine, being careful not to overmix (do not use a mixer). Fold in the apples and nuts.

4 Pour the batter into the baking dish.

5 Bake for 35 to 45 minutes, until the top is golden brown and a toothpick inserted into the center comes out clean. Enjoy with vanilla ice cream and/or whipped cream on top.

ORANGE PINEAPPLE CAKE

Picture this, buddy: You're eight years old playing at the beach all day and you come home to a cold orange pineapple cake in the fridge. Quite the vibe, eh? Now enjoy it every day as an adult.

SERVES 12

Nonstick cooking spray
One 11-ounce can mandarin oranges
½ cup vegetable oil
4 eggs
One 15.25-ounce box yellow butter cake mix

Topping

One 16-ounce can crushed pineapple
12 ounces whipped topping, such as Cool Whip
One 3.4-ounce box instant vanilla pudding

1   Preheat the oven to 350°F and spray a 9 x 13-inch baking pan with cooking spray. Strain the oranges, saving the juice.

2   **Make the cake:** In a large bowl, whisk together the vegetable oil, orange juices, and eggs.

3   In another large bowl, toss the oranges in the cake mix to coat. Add this mixture to the bowl with the wet ingredients and gently incorporate.

4   Bake for 30 minutes, until the cake is golden brown on top and a toothpick comes out clean. Set aside to cool.

5   **Make the topping:** In a medium bowl, mix together the pineapple with the juice, whipped topping, and pudding mix.

6   Spread over top of the cooled cake and enjoy!

BLUEBERRY COFFEE CAKE

Wake everyone up to the aroma of this sweet breakfast cake, bursting with blueberries and topped with cinnamon crumble. It's best enjoyed in the summer when blueberries are in season, but you can also make it year-round with frozen berries. Pair with a cup of fresh jitter juice.

SERVES 12

Nonstick cooking spray
2 cups all-purpose flour
¾ cup sugar
2½ teaspoons baking powder
½ teaspoon kosher salt
¾ cup milk
¼ cup melted vegetable shortening, such as Crisco
1 egg
2 cups fresh blueberries

Topping
⅓ cup all-purpose flour
½ cup sugar
½ teaspoon ground cinnamon
4 tablespoons (½ stick) butter, softened

1 Preheat the oven to 350°F. Spray a 9 x 13-inch baking dish with cooking spray.

2 **Make the cake:** In a large bowl, mix the flour, sugar, baking powder, and salt.

3 In another large bowl, mix the milk, shortening, and egg. Add the dry ingredients and gently mix to combine. Fold in the blueberries.

4 **Make the topping:** In a medium bowl, mix the flour, sugar, and cinnamon. Use a fork to mash the butter into the mixture, forming a crumbly texture. Crumble the topping over the batter.

5 Bake for 45 minutes, until a toothpick inserted into the center comes out clean. Enjoy!

BROWN SUGAR & NUT CAKE

Made famous by my Aunt Martha, this recipe was thoughtfully packaged and shipped right to our doorstep for the holidays and special occasions. Whether as a dessert, snack, or breakfast treat, this cake is versatile and can be enjoyed any time of the day. The rich flavor of brown sugar and the savory crunch of nuts are paired best with jitter juice, tea, or a cold glass of milk.

SERVES 9

Nonstick cooking spray
1 cup all-purpose flour
1 cup granulated sugar
1 teaspoon baking soda
½ teaspoon kosher salt
1 cup fruit cocktail in heavy syrup
1 egg
3 tablespoons brown sugar, or to taste
½ cup chopped nuts, such as pecans
Whipped cream

1 Preheat the oven to 350°F. Spray a 9-inch square baking dish with cooking spray.

2 In a large bowl, sift together the flour, sugar, baking soda, and salt.

3 Add the fruit cocktail and egg and mix well.

4 Transfer the batter to the baking dish, then sprinkle with the brown sugar and chopped nuts.

5 Bake for 40 to 45 minutes, until the top is nicely browned and crunchy.

6 Top with whipped cream and enjoy!

CARROT CAKE

Sneak in those veggies with this carrot-packed dessert. It's a classic carrot cake, perfected with just the right spice mixture, a crunch of pecans, and a homemade cozy blanket of cream cheese frosting over the top. This very carrot cake won the great Boy Scout bake-offs of '96 and '97 and controversially placed second in 1998.

SERVES 6

Nonstick cooking spray
1⅓ cups all-purpose flour
1 cup granulated sugar
1 teaspoon baking powder
1 teaspoon ground cinnamon, plus more for serving
½ teaspoon ground ginger
½ teaspoon kosher salt
¼ teaspoon ground nutmeg
3 eggs
1 cup vegetable oil
2 teaspoons vanilla extract
3 carrots, grated (about 1 cup)
½ cup pecans
½ cup raisins

Frosting
4 ounces cream cheese, softened
4 tablespoons (½ stick) butter, softened
1¼ cup powdered sugar
1 teaspoon heavy cream
1 teaspoon vanilla extract

1 Preheat the oven to 350°F. Spray a 9 x 5-inch loaf pan with cooking spray.

2 **Make the cake:** In a large bowl, whisk the flour, granulated sugar, baking powder, cinnamon, ginger, salt, and nutmeg.

3 Add the eggs, vegetable oil, and vanilla and mix well.

4 Carefully fold in the carrots, pecans, and raisins.

5 Bake for 50 to 60 minutes, until the top is golden brown and a toothpick inserted into the center comes out clean. Set aside and let cool.

6 **Make the frosting:** In a large bowl, mix the cream cheese, butter, powdered sugar, heavy cream, and vanilla until smooth and creamy.

7 Spread the frosting over top of the cooled cake, sprinkle with cinnamon, and enjoy!

GRANDMA'S REESE'S BARS

These bars, made by my grandmother, introduced me to one of the greatest combinations of all time: peanut butter and chocolate. Every time she made them, I would sneak into the kitchen late at night for one more bar with a glass of cold chocolate milk. These bars have been one of my favorite desserts for a long time, and I think they'll quickly become one of yours, too.

MAKES 25 BARS

1 generous cup peanut butter
5 cups powdered sugar
1 cup brown sugar
1 cup butter (2 sticks), softened
1 teaspoon vanilla extract

Topping
4 tablespoons (½ stick) butter
2 cups chocolate chips

1 **Make the bars:** In a large bowl, combine the peanut butter, powdered sugar, brown sugar, softened butter, and vanilla.

2 Press the mixture into the bottom of a 9 x 13-inch baking dish.

3 **Make the topping:** Place the butter in a medium microwaveable bowl. Microwave for 20 seconds to melt, then add the chocolate chips and stir until the chocolate is melted and creamy (see Tip).

4 Pour the chocolate mixture over top of the peanut butter mixture.

5 Set in the fridge to cool for 3 to 4 hours. Slice and enjoy!

Tip: If the chocolate isn't melting, microwave in 15-second intervals, stirring in between.

GRANDPA BOB'S FUDGE

Grandpa Bob perfected this fudge over years of trial and error. He finally got it right with a calibrated candy thermometer and some patience. This fudge recipe is well worth the effort; it's sure to satisfy a sweet tooth.

MAKES ABOUT 50 PIECES

4 cups sugar
2 cups half and half
3 tablespoons light corn syrup, such as Karo
¼ cup cocoa powder
¼ teaspoon kosher salt
4 tablespoons (½ stick) butter, softened
2 teaspoons vanilla extract
½ cup chopped pecans
Nonstick cooking spray

1 In a medium saucepan, mix the sugar, half and half, corn syrup, cocoa powder, and salt.

2 Cook very slowly over low heat until a candy thermometer reads 235°F, about 2 hours. Make sure to scrape the sides of the saucepan so the mixture doesn't stick to the sides.

3 Remove from the heat and, without stirring, add the butter and vanilla. Let sit until a thermometer reads 140°F.

4 Start beating the mixture thoroughly until some of the gloss is gone and the mixture starts to thicken slightly. Stir in the nuts.

5 Spray an 8-inch square flex cake pan with cooking spray. Transfer the fudge mixture to the pan and set aside to cool completely, about 1 hour.

6 Flex the pan slightly and the fudge should pop out in one piece. Slice into pieces and enjoy!

MISTAKE COOKIES

My grandmother crafted this recipe entirely by mistake in 1995 while trying to bake a different cookie. It turned out delicious. The recipe stuck and has been a family favorite ever since. She would keep the cookies in an old vanilla ice cream bucket, layered with parchment paper and a piece of white bread to keep them fresh. Serve with a glass of milk and a lot of love, buddy.

MAKES 12 COOKIES

3 cups all-purpose flour
1 teaspoon baking soda
½ teaspoon salt
8 tablespoons (1 stick) butter, softened
1 cup sugar
2 eggs
2 tablespoons whole milk
2 teaspoons vanilla extract

1   Preheat the oven to 375°F. Line a baking sheet with parchment paper.

2   In a medium bowl, mix the flour, baking soda, and salt.

3   In a large bowl, beat the butter and sugar until light and fluffy. Add the eggs one at a time, mixing until combined. Stir in the milk and vanilla and gently mix to form a dough.

4   Divide into 2-inch balls and place, evenly spaced, on the baking sheet. Use a fork to press down on each ball in a crosshatch pattern.

5   Bake for 9 minutes, until they are just starting to brown on top. Enjoy!

HOMEMADE CHOCOLATE PUDDING

This isn't your average lunch box cup of pudding, buddy. The secret ingredient is the instant coffee that gives it a bold and sharp flavor. You'll never not make it from scratch again.

SERVES 8

4 cups whole milk
1½ cups sugar
¾ cup unsweetened cocoa powder
½ cup cornstarch
1 teaspoon instant coffee
½ teaspoon kosher salt
4 tablespoons (½ stick) butter
1½ teaspoons vanilla extract

1 To a medium saucepan over medium heat, add the milk, sugar, cocoa powder, cornstarch, coffee, and salt. Whisk until smooth.

2 Simmer and cook until the mixture thickens and coats the back of a spoon, stirring constantly for 2 to 3 minutes.

3 Remove from the heat. Add the butter and vanilla, then stir until smooth.

4 Pour into a container, then press plastic wrap on top of the pudding.

5 Place in the fridge for a few hours, then serve cold. Enjoy!

DRINKS

HUG IN A MUG
(HOT COCOA)

Like a warm hug, this cocoa warms you up on a cold night. Top with marshmallows or whipped cream and share a few mugs with your best buddies.

SERVES 2

2 cups milk
½ cup grated milk chocolate
2 heaping tablespoons cocoa powder
2 tablespoons honey
1 cinnamon stick
Whipped cream, for serving

1   To a small saucepan over medium heat, add the milk, chocolate, cocoa powder, honey, and cinnamon stick.

2   Let simmer until steaming, 5 to 7 minutes, until the chocolate is melted and all of the ingredients are incorporated. Remove the cinnamon stick.

3   Pour into a mug, top with whipped cream, and enjoy!

FIRESIDE APPLE CIDER

An autumn tradition. Nothing brings in the crisp autumn season like homemade cider over the fire. Make a big pot of this cider and watch the leaves fall.

MAKES 1 GALLON

16 cups water
5 Gala apples, quartered
5 Honeycrisp apples, quartered
1 large orange, halved
¾ cup brown sugar
1 tablespoon ground allspice
1 tablespoon ground cinnamon
6 cinnamon sticks
Apple slices, for serving

1   Add the water to a large stockpot and place on a grate over the fire.

2   Add the apples and oranges to the pot.

3   Mix in the brown sugar, allspice, ground cinnamon, and cinnamon sticks.

4   Bring to a simmer and cover with a lid. Maintain the fire and simmer for 2 to 3 hours, until the apples are very soft and falling apart.

5   Stir well, then carefully mash the apples with a potato masher. Strain the apple cider through a fine-mesh sieve. Discard the solids and strain again if needed.

6   Serve warm with a slice of apple on top and enjoy!

BUTTERSCOTCH STEAMER

Can't sleep, eh? This butterscotch steamer is the perfect nightcap to help you drift off to dreamland. Pair with *Fritz's Field Notes* for a relaxing evening.

SERVES 4

4 cups milk
¼ cup brown sugar
2 tablespoons salted butter
Ground cinnamon

1 In a medium saucepan, heat the milk over medium-low heat until steaming hot, 6 to 7 minutes. Do not bring to a boil.

2 Remove from the heat and whisk in the brown sugar and butter. Stir until the butter melts and the sugar dissolves.

3 Serve warm in a mug, topped with a sprinkle of cinnamon. Enjoy!

SLOW COOKER MULLED WINE

Cranberries, honey, orange, and spices make this mulled wine a favorite for the holiday season. The smell of this drink will get you in the spirit and warm your whole being from the inside out.

SERVES 8

Two 750 ml bottles red wine

½ cup brandy

1 cup fresh cranberries

½ cup honey

Peels from 1 orange

4 cinnamon sticks, plus more
   for serving

2½ tablespoons star anise extract or
   8 star anise pods

1 tablespoon whole cloves

Orange slices, for serving

1 Add the wine, brandy, cranberries, honey, orange peels, cinnamon sticks, star anise extract, and cloves to a slow cooker. Stir to combine.

2 Cook on low heat for 1 hour, until the mixture is warm, sweet, and flavored with the spices.

3 Strain the mulled wine through a fine mesh strainer and discard the orange peels and spices.

4 Serve warm with a fresh orange slice and a cinnamon stick. Enjoy!

SLOW COOKER PUMPKIN WHITE HOT CHOCOLATE

This hot chocolate is great to serve at your annual Halloween potluck. It combines the rich flavor of white chocolate with the earthy sweetness of pumpkin. This is no ordinary hot chocolate.

SERVES 4

4 cups milk

One 15-ounce can pumpkin puree

One 14-ounce can sweetened condensed milk

1 cup white chocolate chips

1 teaspoon pumpkin pie spice, plus more for serving

Whipped cream, for serving

1 Add the milk, pumpkin puree, condensed milk, white chocolate chips, and pumpkin pie spice to a slow cooker and whisk to combine well.

2 Cook on high for 3 hours, stirring every so often to melt the chocolate.

3 Set the slow cooker to warm.

4 Serve with whipped cream on top and sprinkle with more pumpkin pie spice. Enjoy!

BANANA SPLIT SMOOTHIE

Dust off the old kitchen blender and fill it with fresh fruit. When you want the taste of an ice cream dessert but don't want the ice cream, this banana split smoothie is a sweet alternative that tastes even better than the iconic ice cream version.

SERVES 1 TO 2

2 cups frozen strawberries
1 large banana, sliced
1 cup chocolate milk
¾ cup plain Greek yogurt
1 tablespoon honey

For Serving
Whipped cream
Maraschino cherries with stems

1   Add the strawberries, banana, chocolate milk, yogurt, and honey to a blender and blend until smooth.

2   Serve with whipped cream and a cherry or two on top. Enjoy!

KEY LIME MILKSHAKE

Picture eating a slice of grandma's homemade key lime pie down in Florida. This recipe brings the tropical flavors home to make into your own tall milkshake. I like to make it in the winter months to remind me that warmer days are just ahead. Enjoy with your favorite video game, buddy.

SERVES 6

4 cups vanilla ice cream

½ cup graham cracker crumbs, plus more for serving

¼ cup sweetened condensed milk

¼ cup key lime juice

1 teaspoon honey

½ teaspoon lime zest, plus more for serving

Whipped cream, for serving

1   Add the ice cream, graham cracker crumbs, condensed milk, key lime juice, honey, and lime zest to a blender and blend until smooth.

2   Serve immediately in a tall glass with a straw, topped with whipped cream, a sprinkle of graham cracker crumbs, and lime zest. Enjoy!

PEACH LEMONADE

When I was a kid, I spent my summer days running outside, dipping in the creek, and playing under the trees. My mother always had a large pitcher full of ice and this peach lemonade in the fridge. Fresh, juicy peaches mixed with tart lemonade made for the most refreshing, sweet treat after a long day in the hot sun. Every gulp of this drink will bring you back to the tastes of a 90s summer.

SERVES 4

5 cups water
3 peaches, peeled and cubed (see Tip)
¾ cup sugar
Juice of 8 lemons (about 1 cup)
Peach and lemon slices, for serving

1 Add the water to a large saucepan and bring to a boil. Add the peaches and sugar and boil until the sugar dissolves, 1 to 2 minutes, stirring constantly.

2 Transfer the mixture to a blender and blend on high until smooth.

3 Pour the mixture through a strainer into a pitcher. Press the peach pulp against the strainer to make sure you get all of the juice out. Move the pitcher to the fridge to chill for 45 to 60 minutes.

4 Remove from the fridge, then add the lemon juice into the pitcher. Stir well to combine.

5 Serve over lots of ice with peach and lemon slices. Enjoy!

Tip: To peel peaches easily, score the top of each peach with an X. Bring a pot of water to a boil, add the peaches, and blanch for 30 seconds. Immediately rinse in ice cold water, and the peel should slide right off.

HONEY CINNAMON COLD BREW

I'm no stranger to a hot cup of classic jitter juice, but I do like to mix it up sometimes with a crafted cold brew. Fresh local honey and a sprinkle of cinnamon are the perfect companions for that after-dinner cup of jitter juice.

SERVES 4

1 cup coffee grounds
4 cups cold water
¼ cup honey
¼ cup warm water
2 cups whole milk
¼ teaspoon ground cinnamon, plus more for serving

1 In a pitcher, combine the coffee grounds and cold water. Mix well, then refrigerate overnight or for at least 12 hours.

2 Using a fine mesh strainer with a coffee filter over top, strain the coffee into another pitcher.

3 To a small bowl, add the honey and warm water. Mix well until the honey dissolves, then stir in the cinnamon.

4 Pour 1 cup of cold brewed coffee into a tall glass filled with ice, then add 2 tablespoons of the honey syrup and ½ cup of milk. Sprinkle with cinnamon. Enjoy!

INDEX